Design Dialogue

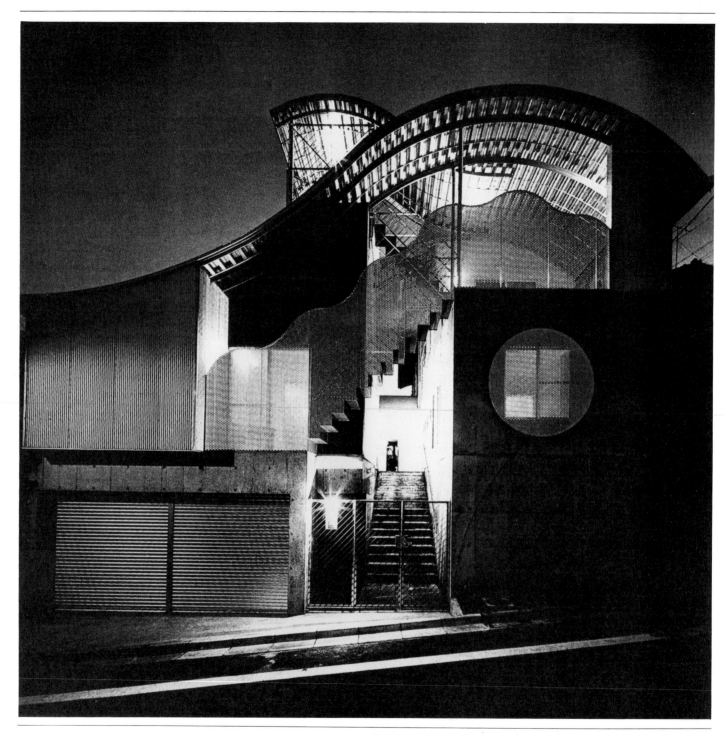

Celebrating the human spirit, designers seek highly individual and creative solutions. Itsuko Hasagawa's residential design in Tokyo exemplifies innovative thinking.

Design Dialogue

Jack Stoops

Formerly U.C.L.A., University of Washington

Jerry Samuelson

California State University, Fullerton

Davis Publications, Inc., Worcester, Massachusetts

Acknowledgments

Special recognition and gratitude go to Kazuo Kuwabara who contributed generously of his time and talent to this book; he took many of the photographs and meticulously rendered the charts, design diagrams and color scheme compositions.

Dextra Frankel has been generous in allowing us to photograph many design examples from her personal art collection.

Russell Thurston, California State University, Fullerton staff photographer, assisted in the processing and custom printing of many of the photographs.

Finally we are most grateful to the designers and museums for graciously allowing work to be included, and to all who gave encouragement and assistance toward the completion of this book.

Copyright 1990
Davis Publications, Inc.
Worcester, Massachusetts U.S.A.

Printed in the United States of America
Library of Congress Catalog Card Number:
ISBN: 0-87192-225-8

Graphic Design: Jerry Samuelson

10   9   8   7   6   5   4   3   2   1

Contents

Foreword 1

Introduction 3

Part I Perception and Imagination 5

   Chapter 1 Visual Awareness: Expanding the Perceptive Eye 9
     Practical Vision, Curious Vision, Imaginative Vision, Pure Vision

   Chapter 2 Visual Research: Expanding the Individual Experience 15
     Environmental Images, Recorded Images

   Chapter 3 Visual Imagination: The Creation of a New Image 23
     Selection, Alteration, Spontaneity, Abstraction, Nonfigurative Images

Part II A Visual Vocabulary 33

   Chapter 4 The Image: Definition and Structure 35
     Line, Value, Color, Shape and Form, Texture, Space

   Chapter 5 The Image: Interaction and Order 73
     Proportion, Emphasis, Movement, Balance, Repetition

Part III Design Process 87

   Chapter 6 Response and Expression 88
     Motivation, Expression, Materials, Function, Symbolism

   Chapter 7 A Strategy for Problem Solving 111
     Recognition of the Problem, Spontaneous Trials, Research, Clarification, Refinement, Resolution

Part IV Design Influences 115

   Chapter 8 Design in Transition 117
     Victorian, Art Nouveau, Art Deco, Bauhaus and the Modern Movement, Post-Modern

   Chapter 9 Design Innovators 149
     Michael Thonet, William Morris, Louis Comfort Tiffany, Arthur H. Mackmurdo, Alphonse Mucha, Henry van de Velde, Charles R. Mackintosh, Aubrey Beardsley, Eileen Gray, Ludwig Mies van der Rohe, Joseph Albers, Johannes Itten, Raymond Loewy, Marianne Brandt, Lazlo Moholy-Nagy, Ben Shahn, Anni Albers, Herbert Bayer, A. M. Cassandre, Marcel Breuer, Henry Dreyfus, Gyorgy Kepes, Alexander Girard, Charles and Ray Eames, George Nelson, Hans Wegner, Paul Rand, Florence Schust Knoll Bassett, Ettore Sottsass, Herb Lubalin, Saul Bass, Jack Lenor Larsen, Seymour Chwast, Milton Glaser, Ikko Tanaka

Part V Design Projects 189

Every artifact in the environment has been designed, from postage stamps to space stations. Sometimes a design is developed intuitively by a craftsperson seeking a solution to a problem. Most often solutions are the result of conscious efforts of designers striving to solve both functional and aesthetic aspects of a problem.

DESIGN is both process and product. As process, design is visual problem solving: creating, organizing, and evaluating. As product, design is a tangible visual solution. It is a resolution of visual elements, materials, and function expressing the unique personal stamp of the designer.

While it is true that design is an integral part of all visual art, this book focuses on functional design that seeks to create aesthetic solutions to visual problems touching the daily lives of everyone.

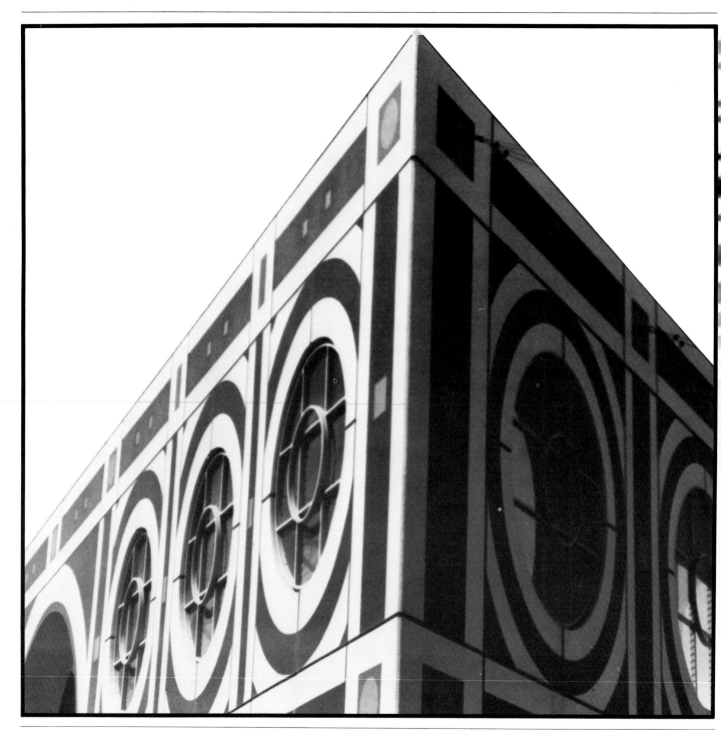

2

The dramatic impact of bold visual forms used by architect Jon Jerde in his plan of the Horton Plaza Mall expresses a new vigor in design expression.

Introduction

An aspiring student of design is called upon to learn a large number of skills, historical data, bits of technical information, attitudes, and sensitivities. The purpose of this book is to set forth the major considerations in a succinct, clear manner. The authors are keenly aware that many of a designer's best thoughts are nonverbal; as the writing progressed we realized that words often failed to express our intent precisely. Such hazards persist when writing about visual matters, but the visuals here should help to clarify the text. Although reliance on words is necessary, the essential content, and intent, is *visual.*

To function effectively, the creative designer is required to understand and use a visual vocabulary (basic design elements), and to be critically aware of all visual relationships created: color to color, line to line, value to value, textural passages and spacing. Rudolf Arnheim, psychologist and art scholar, calls this kind of visual sensitivity *visual thinking* — a skill that can surely be developed with diligent practice. The ability is quite different from intellectual thought.

The potential for visual thinking is present, but often dampened and perhaps even extinguished by years of education emphasizing verbal skills and logical, rational thought. A restoration of a nice balance between thinking and feeling becomes the goal. At times the designer must think clearly on a rational, logical level using the left hemisphere of the brain; yet during the problem-solving phases of design, intuition is called upon, using the brain's right hemisphere. The interplay between the two sides of the brain often provides a sudden flash of creative energy called insight. It is such dynamic interaction that the designer must learn to activate. At these exciting moments, the whole individual works in harmony; deficiencies in one capacity are balanced by strengths in another. Insight grows, of course, as experience expands. Visual images, information, and ideas are all stored in the visual memory bank. The designer needs to be surrounded with objects and images that nourish inner resources. New images will coalesce as one learns to rely upon and to activate the right side of the brain.

Of great value, also, is a well-developed plan of approach; a way of working that will open pathways to solving design problems. The development of a fruitful plan of action will be a highly individual matter. Some suggestions for strategies are set forth in chapter 7.

Various chapters describe ideal growth progressions that may not be achieved easily. A combination of calm reflection and hard work can lead to success. However, true competence develops slowly, and surely not in a predictable order or with various competencies maturing at an even rate. Information about famous designers and major design movements stimulates growth and insight. A knowledge of the thought processes that produced and shaped the historically recent nineteenth-century Arts and Crafts movement, Art Nouveau, Bauhaus, and Art Deco contributes to a growing understanding of design evolution.

As with all hard work, there is a resulting joy and deep satisfaction that comes with conceiving an idea and shepherding it through to completion. Imaginative and dedicated designers are needed to help solve the difficult visual problems of our twentieth-century environment.

Part I

Perception and Imagination

Perception and imagination—a pair of potent mental attributes that provide energy for the designer. While some artists seem to function intuitively, others may have to reach out consciously to activate their perception and imagination.

What are the meanings inherent in the term *imagination?* Imagination is the inner force that allows one to experience what was, what can be, and what might never be; it can transcend the limitations of space, time, and reality. Sometimes imagination may be a leap into fantasy, often expressed through dreams that reflect inner thoughts and desires. But imagination is more than involuntary illusion; it allows voluntary turning of ideas in the mind, trying new combinations, uncovering unexpected insights through a conscious guiding

of visual invention. Imagination not only allows the picturing in the mind's eye of the earth as a sphere floating in space, it can also provide such inventions as Lewis Carroll's Jabberwock—"Beware the Jabberwock, my son! The jaws that bite, the claws that catch!"

Original imagery is often experienced in night dreams or in daydreams. Rudolf Arnheim writes in *Art and Visual Perception* that during sleep the human mind seems to descend to a more elementary level at which life situations are described not by abstract concepts but by significant images. This creative imagination, often liberated in sleep, is the power of picture language from which the artist draws.[1] The designer need not depend entirely upon sleep to liberate images, but seeks awareness of inner imagery while awake. In

1 Rudolf Arnheim, *Art and Visual Perception*, p. 142.

5

6

Upper left: A real tiger — the stimulus for three imaginative images.
Upper right: Detail; London Transport poster.
Lower left: Detail; Mexican yarn design.
Lower right: Logo design, Hungry Tiger Restaurants.

his book *Experiences in Visual Thinking,* Robert McKim suggests some conditions to foster inner imagery: a quiet environment, relaxed attention, and a desire to see.[2]

Imagination is clearly an essential part of the design process, bringing imaginative power into harmony with the perceptive eye.

Perception is visual intake that nourishes and stimulates the imagination; raw visual material is experienced, stored, and later may rise to consciousness in time of creative need. Louis Pasteur pointed out that invention springs from the prepared mind. Visual perception is the source of preparation for the designer. Perception is the mental grasp of objects or images through the senses leading to insight or intuition. True visual perception requires attention, effort, work, practice, concentration, and serious commitment. Clearly, perception extends well beyond mere recognition and identification in which a shoe is seen, a cat recognized, a penny found in the street. Quick visual intake is pertinent to our momentary needs and to little else. To see only on this elementary level leads to visual poverty. Visual perception moves the eye from casual looking to penetrating observation and, as visual skills are developed, to intensified seeing that involves a high degree of attention and concentration. In breaking out of visual poverty, the designer discovers a wealth of stimulating images and savors the intrinsic visual qualities of every conceivable object in the environment: shells, cloud formations, puddles, shadow shapes, light patterns. Frank Barron, educational psychologist, has pointed out a close relationship between per-

2 Robert McKim, *Experiences in Visual Thinking,* p. 46.

An imaginary image invented by Sir John Tenniel for Lewis Carrol's *Through the Looking Glass..*

7

ception and intuition; his research clearly reveals the perceptual sources of supposedly covert, hidden, intuitive thought.

The study of visual perception has intrigued psychologists; yet many of their studies delve into influences affecting perceptions that have only peripheral relevance to aesthetic visual perception. M. D. Vernon[3] describes studies of visual perception dealing with speed and accuracy of perception, and the influences of such distractions as pain, hunger, noise, attention factors, and selection.

Of these influences, selection is especially useful to the designer in the visual arts. Surrounded by millions of possible stimuli, the designer must select and focus on specific images and relegate others to the periphery of the visual field.

8

3 M. D. Vernon, *The Psychology of Perception*, p. 79.

The educated eye explores the visual qualities of a group of shells. The perceptive eye first identifies a flower and then continues on to enjoy light and shape variations.

Chapter 1

Visual Awareness: Expanding the Perceptive Eye

More than basic selection is involved in aesthetic perception. Beyond discrimination and selection there is another level of attention. An object is explored for intrinsic visual qualities, i.e., shapes are examined for size, joining, turning, tapering, and intersecting; surfaces are scanned for textures, colors, patterns, and light modulations. It is precisely this kind of visual attention that John Dewey had in mind when he wrote:

> To think effectively in terms of relations of qualities is as severe a demand upon thought as to think in terms of symbols, verbal and mathematical. Indeed, since words are easily manipulated in mechanical ways, the production of a work of genuine art probably demands more intelligence than does most of the so-called thinking that goes on among those who pride themselves on being intellectuals.[4]

Intensified visual perception is a form of thinking—a kind often overlooked, unrecognized, and misunderstood. Rudolf Arnheim supports the concept of visual perception as intelligence:

> My contention is that the cognitive operations called thinking are not the privilege of mental processes above and beyond perception but the essential ingredients of perception itself.[5]

For the designer, the act of perception is the vital link to visual growth, imaginative power, and aesthetic intuition. An examination of levels of seeing described by Ralph Pearson, art educator, may be useful in increasing perceptive awareness.[6]

---

4 John Dewey, *Art as Experience*, p. 46.
5 Rudolf Arnheim, *Visual Thinking*, p. 13.
6 Ralph Pearson, *How to See Modern Pictures*, p. 33.

9

10

Imaginative vision results in an unexpected combination of familiar images. Artist: Milton Glaser.

Pearson outlines four main kinds of vision:

1. Practical vision
2. Curious vision
3. Imaginative or reflective vision
4. Pure vision

Practical Vision — Vision that results in action is practical vision. A bus approaches and one steps onto the curb for safety. Objects are located to be used in daily activities: knobs, buttons, coins, utensils, and discursive symbols, e.g. STOP, GO, CAUTION. This kind of vision is practical indeed, for without it survival would be difficult. It is object oriented; it labels and classifies for use.

Curious Vision — Curious vision involves a slight shift from practical vision. After quick identification has been established, one examines an object to determine some information about it, e.g., How old is it? Of what is it made? Where was it made? How does it fit together? A person who habitually uses vision for practical purposes to recognize budget figures, schedules, graphs, weights, and so on will often display added interest in an object: a redwood burl, a Persian knife, an ancient coin. This is curious vision characterized by close, intense observation rarely bestowed on familiar, ordinary functional objects. It is less rapid than practical vision where light-

ning-like recognition occurs. Scientific observation is an ultimate refinement and control of curious vision; yet the most disciplined scientific eye may remain blind to intrinsic, visual patterns and configurations. For example, an anthropologist identifying Zuni pottery, design motifs, and ethnological symbolism may remain utterly blind to the pottery's aesthetic qualities.

Imaginative or Reflective Vision — This kind of vision engages powers of visual recall. One recreates in the "mind's eye" a certain object, person, or experience. A creative leap forward allows the mind to engage in a new level of invention in which images are not only recalled but mixed through free play of the imagination. Astonishing images evolve from this kind of seeing.

Pure Vision — In pure vision objects are observed for their intrinsic visual qualities, disconnected from all practical associations. A rusty tin can or a peeling signboard may be of more interest than a precious stone. In pure vision the eye sees the peeling signboard and the precious stone for what they actually are: forms, subtle shifts of values as light plays on their surfaces, textures, and colors. All other considerations are set aside, and the pure visual impression is allowed to enter con-

Upper: Practical vision is called into constant use as daily tasks, such as tying a shoe, are performed.
Middle: Curious vision is used to identify the microscopic image of a young female cone of *Pinus excelsa*.

Lower: Pure vision recognizes the dried seed pod and moves on quickly to enjoy the twisted, textured formation.

sciousness. Literally one is set free to see, to experience all sorts of images regardless of setting, cost, prior associations, etc.—pure vision is liberated vision. When vision is liberated fully, true visual perception begins.

Both historical and contemporary design reveal a pervasive interaction of perception and imagination.

Attraction and close examination of a snail shell and/or the chambered nautilus undoubtedly provided the motivation for the ever-expanding curve of the scroll or the spiral design form that appears in several variations in Greek art. Greek designers chose to modify, join, repeat, and adjust the coiling spiral to suit a number of design uses.

A contemporary designer, Erik Nitsche, responded visually to the fleeting, flashing images one perceives while riding in a subway train. His design for a subway poster captures the rush of movement and color, fusing the impressions into an imaginative and striking visual statement.

The two examples cited provide evidence of a relationship between visual source and design solution. The designer may not leave such unmistakable tracks; an idea may be reworked until it bears little resemblance to the original visual stimulus. Then

too sources and visual cues may undergo a long period of gestation during which the designer may forget the original stimulus. The designer practices perceptual openness; he or she is forever perceiving and absorbing environmental stimuli and storing images that fuel creative endeavors.

The following chapters explore specific ways of exercising perception and liberating imaginative powers.

Upper: A hub-cap provides the eye with an interesting array of fractured reflections.
Middle: Intersecting gears form complex visual relationships.

Lower: Speed, movement, and flashing images like those seen on a subway ride have been created by artist Erik Nitsche for a New York subway poster.

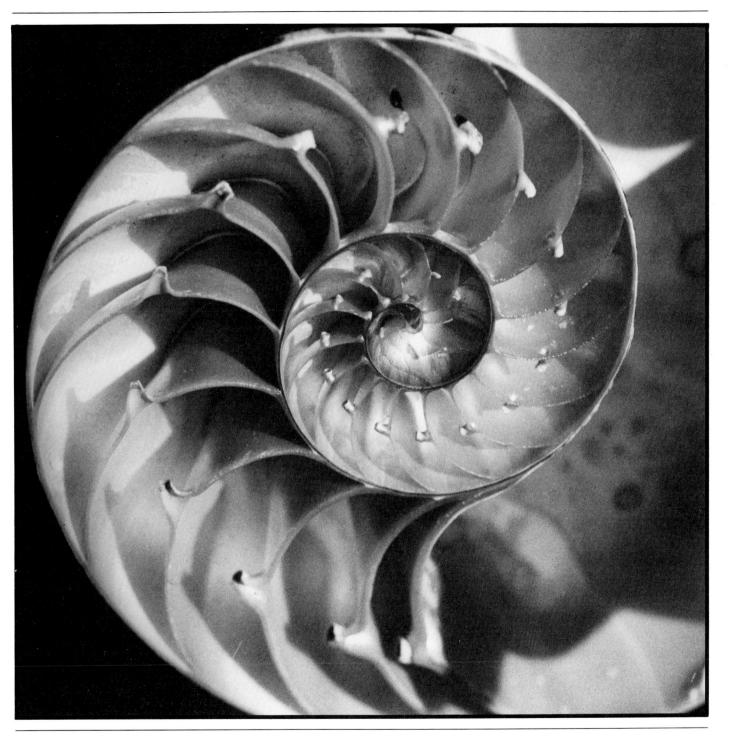

The spiral line of the chambered nautilus and the light and shadow variations in each chamber delight the eye.

13

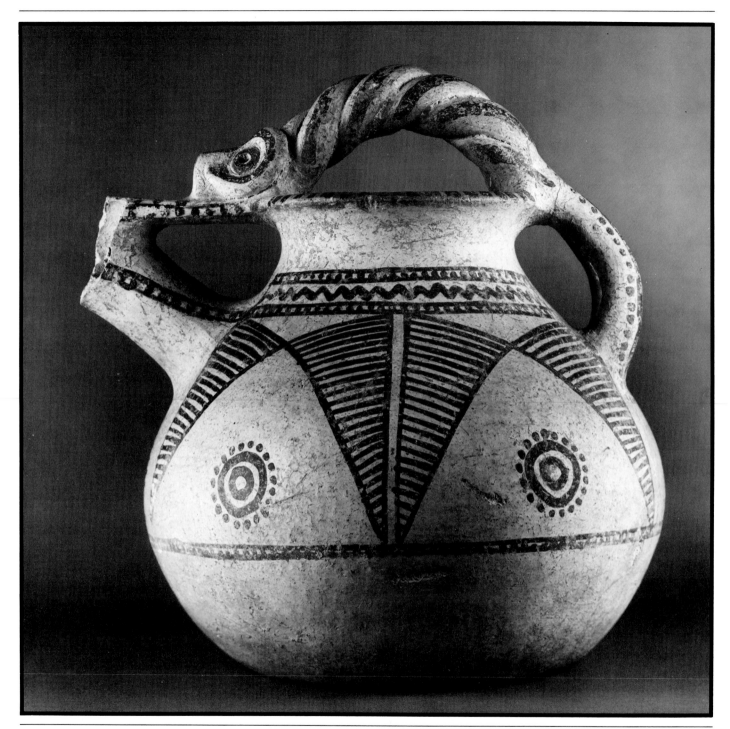

14

Historical examples enrich the designer's visual intake. This ancient
Luristan vessel (850-780 B.C.) shows refinement of form, restrained
linear enrichment and an imaginative yet intrinsic handling of an animal
figure.

Chapter 2

Visual Research: Expanding the Individual Experience

In the opening to part I and the previous chapter, two key human attributes were discussed: perception and imagination. These human capabilities are essential for artistic problem solving, and the designer is called upon to exercise and develop both.

As with any latent human potential, exercise is essential to ensure growth and to prevent atrophy. Muscles, memory, speech, vision: all may be developed to astounding capacity provided a strenuous regimen is established and followed.

Many books and manuals describe programs for development of physical prowess. Much less has been written and prescribed for the development of perception and imagination. Some guidance for designers is set forth in this chapter.

A student of design needs to develop a psychological readiness to perceive the environment in an aesthetic way. Perception and aesthetic attention are intimately linked. Fortunately, the first engenders the second, revealing a close relationship in experience. (It is interesting to note that the term *aesthetic* is derived from the Greek word *aisthesis,* meaning "perception," which suggests that expanding one's visual intake will in turn sensitize one to visual qualities.) Perceptual experience leads to aesthetic growth; it involves becoming more discerning and aware of the existence, the character, and the ever-varying qualities of things out there. By looking deeply one often is moved; thus aesthetic response is activated by paying attention to the sensuous dimensions of experience.

When this skill becomes sharpened through conscious self-direction, it may legitimately be called *visual research,* since it is the pursuit of knowledge through systematic inquiry.

In art, the term *knowledge* refers to perceptual intake and experiential storage of aesthetic qualities, not to empirical factual information. To be informed aesthetically differs entirely from memorizing precise data. When one becomes knowledgeable aesthetically, the elusive visual qualities of images will have been absorbed by thoughts and feelings.

At times, the visual experience may be stored in memory or may be recorded with photographs or sketches. In either case, the designer is acquiring a valuable fund of visual information, often impossible to translate into words. Such highly specific visual information residing in images may remain dormant until the active perceptive eye sees it. This energetic seeking and seeing develops what might be called aesthetic intelligence. With a growing sense of aesthetic intelligence, the designer develops strengths to be called upon in solving visual problems. Without a penetrating aesthetic intelligence, the designer's solutions are apt to be superficial or faddish and empty of aesthetic feeling.

The first large realm of visual research is the environment, both natural and human-made.
Environmental Images — Today the visual environment includes normal visual intake as well as telescopic and microscopic images. Much learning of design principles derives from careful observation of the world of images. Drawings by cave artists show the impact of animal forms upon early life and ex-

pression. As civilization developed, human beings built tools, boats, weapons, and shelters, and adorned themselves with jewelry and clothes—which also became a part of the visual environment. These artifacts added to the abundant natural sources of design.

A sense of visual organization, form, structure, and articulation all spring from observation of the world of nature. Discoveries abound in the exploration of such diverse examples as crystals, skeletal forms, crustacea, leaf patterns, and insect life.

A distinction should be made that design success is not mere imitation of nature. Rather, it is the perception and interpretation of proportion, spatial relationships, and shapes found in natural forms that is significant. Analysis of natural structural qualities that occur again and again generates a sensitive aesthetic responsiveness that never deserts one.

Design ideas are more apt to flow from a mind that has been imprinted with rich and varied visual experience rather than one that has had limited exposure. Poverty of idea results from impoverished perceptual intake. Why should such poverty occur when the environment teems with visual images waiting to be claimed? Perhaps the sheer abundance acts as a deterrent at times; surely it is a deterrent until the design student learns the necessary skills to advance beyond idle looking and begins to see perceptively.

Any intensified encounter with stimuli brings on confusion, perhaps even withdrawal as a form of protection from overstimulation. In order to confront a multiplicity of visual

Environmental images: Nature — A rich diversity of shape and detail can be found in a selection of cacti and succulents. Selection and concentration enrich the visual intake.

17

18

Environmental images: Designer-made — The visual environment is filled with objects made by people. A series of autos shows a striking variety of fenders, grills, lights, bumpers, and other design details which can become confusing. Selection and focus are necessary in visual research.

stimuli, the viewer must consciously select, move closer, select again, and eventually focus on individual shapes and forms. The same zeroing in on characteristic detail may be followed while viewing a carnival, a garden, or any segment of the visual environment. Selection and concentration dissipate any feelings of being visually overwhelmed, and soon one senses a steady, calm absorption, enlivened by the excitement of discovery. This is part of the process of visual research as it applies to the environment, both natural and human-made.

Recorded Images — The second area of visual research available to the designer is the wide range of recorded images—images of ancient times and distant places, interpretations by artists, objects of utility, esoteric minutiae, cultural communications, and expressions of timeless beauty. The camera has recorded the visual heritage of all ages, and the printing press has made possible a ready visual reference, accessible at a nearby library or newsstand. Many designers collect a clip file of images taken from magazines and newspapers for quick reference.

The vast trace of history has systematically been researched and published. It is to this recorded source that the designer often looks for accurate visual information. The question may be quite basic: "What are the proportions and details of a Greek temple?" "What is the design detail of a Queen Elizabeth I headdress?" The reference to a single authentic recorded image may be sufficient to unlock the visual answer. The question, however, may be more complex. "What are the visual clues that reveal a specific style such as Art Nouveau or Art Deco?" A more careful search and attention to many examples is necessary to understand the range and variations within a specific style. Depending how the research is to be used, the designer may make sketches of details, take notes, and trace design portions to record essential visual information.

A flood of contemporary images is recorded in current books, magazines, and newspapers. In addition to providing a source of specific images, they may also serve as reference material for examples of page layout, color relationships, and subject interpretations. Of special interest are art magazines, which exhibit the ideas and imaginative solutions of artists around the world. The designer may derive inspiration and encouragement from other artists who are solving contemporary visual problems.

Careful visual research, carried out over a period of years, will allow the designer to accumulate a store of readily available imagery. Relying only on memory may result in generalized minimal imagery, weak in concept and construction. Therefore the young designer at first may need to seek out and record elusive visual information to stimulate imagination and to help generate fresh ideas.

Visual research of recorded images is not a process to be confused with mere copying of imagery; it is a point of departure. First the designer perceives and assimilates the visual information, and then from it creates new imagery.

20

Recorded images: images from historical periods serve as visual reference material stimulating the designer's imagination. Lion's head from ancient Rome.

Upper left: Head of a Maharaja. Folk art in brass from India.
Upper right: Mask of rain god Tlaloc, Mixtec culture, 900-1200 A.D.
Lower left: Head of Orpheus. Coptic fragment, Egypt, fourth or fifth century.
Lower right: Japanese print "Ichikawa Ebizo No Takemura Sadanoshin."
Artist: Toshusai Sharaku, 1794.

21

22

A unique imaginative program design has been created using key objects from the play "The Caretaker." Artist: Cesar Mendoza.

Chapter 3

Visual Imagination: The Creation of a New Image

This discussion focuses directly on visual imagination, aesthetic imagination, creative imagination: the education and refinement of imaginative power. With only a little effort, one can picture the face of the man in the moon. Shadowy shapes perceived on the face of the full moon are mixed in the mind with known human facial features. The result? An imaginary face is seen. Nearly everyone can imagine animal forms, human features, and other objects in clouds, rock formations, and surface stains. Leonardo da Vinci recommended exercising this spontaneous imagining because it limbers up the power to create new ideas.

The designer also learns to tap inner resources, to invent shapes and forms of unknown origin. But more often, one calls upon a store of perceived images built up through the perceptive processes. For the designer, the following five specific strategies for creating new images may be helpful.

Selection — Out of the thousands of images encountered in any given moment, one must choose where to focus—to look at this, rather than that. Physically, selection involves directing sight so that the image strikes the most sensitive region of the retina, the fovea centralis where utmost clarity is registered. The effort required may be called imaginative since it goes beyond the preliminary observation necessary for recognition, and the image at hand is inspected for visual properties.

First a general awareness of the object occurs. It is probable that at this stage identification is made—a familiar face, a door, a book. The next stage is the crucial one: *selection,* which describes the act of taking particular notice, or regarding with attention. With selection comes full, all-out inspection:

1. How a thing looks in profile, full front, from above.
2. How a thing feels, what it weighs.
3. Color variations from top to bottom, side to side, or in different lights.
4. Surface textures and details.
5. The boundaries and/or edges.
6. How a thing is made, how it fits together.
7. How light reveals the form, dark recesses, and light-catching protuberances.

Selection implies that one fully participates in a process of creative forming, an essential step in activating the imagination. Selection operates on two levels: the narrowing of perceptual intake, and the sorting and discarding of ideas to allow a single choice to emerge and mature.

The selection process narrows the field of vision from a general view to a focused view.
Upper: A jumble of tools
Lower: A single tool — crescent wrench.

Alteration — Alteration occurs as soon as the designer begins recording ideas. It is a combination of the recording process itself and a conscious effort to interpret. Sometimes a drawing will result in an exact representation of form or texture. However, even in such a careful rendering, the quality of the medium will be evident and therefore becomes a form of alteration.

Consciously taking liberties, the designer works over sketches, defining edges, emphasizing outlines, exaggerating details, distorting proportions—all imaginative efforts. Alteration is most often a process of simplification. Existing visual elements of form, line, shape, and color may be simplified to clearly express an idea or to unify a presentation. Irregularities may be presented more regularly than on the original, haphazard spots may be changed to patterned spots, color modulation may be changed to flat color. Changes may be subtle variations from the original, or deliberately calculated to create new imagery. A blue apple has dramatic visual impact. The designer purposely alters the familiar to jolt the viewer into taking a second look. Alteration generates new imagery, a result of the interaction of perception and imagination.

The alteration process purposely employs change to develop new imagery.
Upper: A polished apple.
Lower: Apple target.

Spontaneity — At times stubbornly following a single approach may not be the best way to reach for a new idea. Openness and a willingness to break out of the usual patterns, to bring together unrelated elements—to artistically fool around—may be the most productive method of pushing the imagination into action. John Gardner, the psychologist, writes, "The creative process often is not responsive to conscious efforts to initiate or control it. It does not proceed methodically or in programmatic fashion. It meanders. It is unpredictable, digressive, capricious."[7] The alert designer is open to spontaneous ideas and is prepared to jot down notes or make quick sketches. A process to stimulate free flow of thought may be described as a visual brainstorming; the designer records all ideas that occur—good, bad, and in between.

Brainstorming is a way of activating both left and right sides of the brain—the left hemisphere functions logically, rationally, and verbally; intellectual thinking takes place. The right hemisphere is the source of intuitive thinking and feeling. Research indicates that a state of relaxation stimulates right brain activity; thus it is during self-induced relaxation that aesthetic ideas flow.

In this pursuit, it is important not to rule out immediately any unrestrained thoughts, outrageous as they might seem. At some point, however, selection is the key to bringing focus to this process, for without focus one can wander aimlessly, adrift in endless possibilities.

26

7 John Gardner, *Self-Renewal*, p. 34.

Zippered apple.

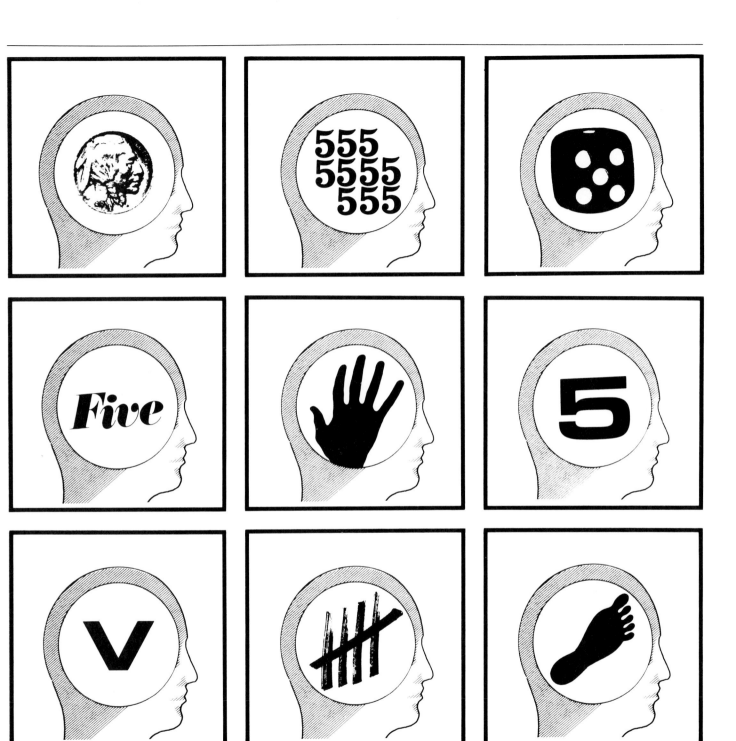

Spontaneity involves the fooling-around approach to reach for new ideas.
A series of image ideas is caught in the mind's eye.

27

Abstraction — Abstraction may be thought of as a form of extraction. Through exercise of the imagination, qualities, proportions, shapes, textures, and colors may be the focus of attention. The process of noticing one aspect and closing off all others is, of course, very close to selection. For example, when a line is used to define the shape of a pear, one aspect of the pear is singled out—the edge. The color, texture, and surface modulation are omitted and the outline shape is extracted. The drawing therefore is an abstraction.

The designer may continue the process of abstraction toward a refined imaginative solution, retaining or eliminating visual information along the way. Abstraction is a continuum, moving further and further away from literal depiction yet always retaining the essence of the perceived image. Abstraction is not withdrawal, not flight from specific concrete experience; rather, it can only be achieved through rich perceptive intake. Rudolph Arnheim observes that "Vision without abstraction is blind; abstraction without vision is empty."[8] Abstract art is not an imperfect attempt to portray nature; it has a positive aesthetic goal clearly observable in world art—African, Egyptian, Oriental, and many others. Abstraction is indispensable to any form of art, be it close to natural form or far removed by the designer's inventiveness.

8 Rudolph Arnheim, *Visual Thinking*, p. 188.

Abstraction is a continuum of change, moving further away from natural appearance.
Upper: From a real duck to a designed wooden duck.

Middle: From a real cat to a designed image.
Lower: From a real butterfly to an abstract butterfly.

29

30

Nonfigurative images contain no reference to perceived objects.
Upper left: Geometric design of a Navajo rug.
Upper right: Top detail of wrought-iron gate. Cambridge University, England.
Lower left: Pottery bowl with linear design. Acoma Tribe, American Indian.
Lower right: Geometric and amorphic shapes are combined in this forged silver, ivory, bone and ebony necklace by Designer/Craftsperson Ramona Solberg.

Nonfigurative Images — Nonfigurative images contain no reference to perceived objects. Such inventions devoid of subject matter may be called pure shape and form, arising directly out of the designer's imagination. Two basic nonfigurative classifications may be noted: geometric and amorphic, as well as combinations of the two. The Moslem design tradition offers a rich compendium of nonfigurative design motifs, since there exist religious prohibitions against portraying human figures. Most cultures combine the figurative and the nonfigurative. Invention of nonfigurative motifs activates free flights of imagination, unhampered by subject demands. There is a great freedom to create a purely "musical" effect; perhaps this category, freed from reference to objects, brings the visual arts close to musical composition where the composer employs melody and rhythm as ends unto themselves.

Today the designer mixes abstract and nonfigurative images to create a highly imaginative blend. Video artists design pure electronic images, making imaginative use of a contemporary medium.

Designers are frequently called upon to create images and compositions that are completely devoid of subject or symbolism. Successful nonfigurative designs display a compelling visual attraction and stand firmly on their own in terms of color, shapes, textures, and lines—nothing more, nothing less.

Upper: Rhythmic linear design on jug, Persia, Kashan, early 13th century.
Lower: A repeat pattern of a decorative Japanese paper.

32

Confronted with a symbol from an unfamiliar language, the eye is liberated from verbal meaning and can concentrate on visual qualities.

Part II

A Visual Vocabulary

To create in any field one must understand that field's essential, basic components. In housing construction, for example, brick, lumber, mortar and nails are the basic materials. Plans are necessary to form these materials into a finished house. The basic ingredients are quite different in music, dance, literature, or art; each discipline requires analysis and dissection to penetrate surface appearances and to grasp the underlying elements comprising the structure.

In art these components are visual, and there exists a well defined vocabulary comprised of line, shape, value, color, and texture. These are the basic visual materials with which the designer creates. However, knowing the vocabulary is not enough. A designer is more than someone who arbitrarily places lines on paper. Instead the design principles of proportion, emphasis, movement, balance and repetition are used to transform the visual vocabulary into coherent, expressive design.

Interaction between the basic visual vocabulary and design principles generates and shapes creative effort. It focuses attention on component parts and increases the designer's conscious control over the work at hand. The designer may be called upon to design a composition of eggs or trees or paper-clips or circles and triangles. The designer must understand aesthetic order which differs from mere orderliness that may result in predictable regularity. Aesthetic order is achieved through unexpected groupings, unpredictable intervals and surprising variation. Thus, the eye is intrigued and delighted by imaginative inven-

33

tion; not bored by dull, pedestrian regularity.

This section will isolate each of the visual elements and principles of design to focus on their specific contribution and to see how they interact in an effective "language of vision."

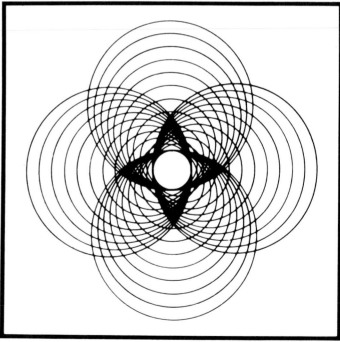

Line can be isolated in the environment — an exercise in pure vision.
Upper: The spider's web is a visual organization of concentric and radiating line.
Lower: A logo design for the Honolulu Symphony Society makes use of multiple intersecting line.

Chapter 4

The Image: Definition and Structure

Six basic elements are studied and used by the designer: line, value, color, texture, shape/form, and space. These are the essential building elements of visual design, giving definition to design images. Each element deserves careful study.

Line — Line records movement, the mark of a pen on paper, a scrawl recorded in wet sand, the trace of a crawling snail, the contrail of a jet. Line, then, is the path of a point moving through space. Diagrams, drawings, symbols, marks, codes, all use line to define and give substance to ideas.

Line is a facile element of the visual vocabulary; it is used to define and describe quickly. Early cave drawings, the pictographs of ancient Egypt, and the linear design on Greek pottery all show early evidence of the importance of line. During the Middle Ages, as monks labored over manuscripts, the linear trace of the pen formed letters of thick and thin line and elaborate linear decoration. Masters of the Renaissance were, first of all, draftsmen. Wood block and metal engravings recorded the etched line drawings of the seventeenth century. Contemporary artists from Picasso to Pollock continued to engage the vitality of line, and today graphic computer printouts extend the potential use of line.

It is somewhat difficult to isolate line for concentrated attention since any line also creates shape and space. A horizontal straight line defines geometric shapes above and below the line. A line that moves, returns, curves, and intersects itself traps and defines complex shapes. Line is visible at the edge of all shapes.

Line is to be found everywhere in nature and to isolate it is an experience in pure vision. Line can be seen in the branches of a barren winter tree, the veining in leaves, the twisting tendrils and gnarled tangles of roots. Lines, in nature, tend to be free flowing, curving, uneven.

The human-made environment also abounds in line, often precise and repetitive. Power lines, crosswalks, signs, edges of geometric buildings, poles, and fences stretch across the landscape. Neon tubes create luminous fluid line, often pulsing with excitement and humor. Careful observation discloses unique differences in human-made line such as found in comparison of a frayed and weathered cable and a sleek plastic-coated one. Humans have also added very personalized line to the landscape. Inner-city streets are often marked with a linear language brashly defining turf.

For the artist, line is often the first element called into the creative process. The preliminary sketch, the doodle, contour drawing, and pattern, may be the first concrete delineation of ideas. A contour line defines the outside shape of an object, boundary lines determine space, repeated lines establish texture, modeling, or pattern. The illusion of space on a flat surface can be achieved by converging lines meeting at a single point on an established horizon line. Line is also used as the understructure, the framework, of an idea.

Line, of course, possesses inherent qualities that contribute significantly to the finished visual image, and at times may be the sole car-

36

Upper: Bare branches create a natural, textured line formation.
Lower: The under structure of stadium seating may be seen as an interplay of vertical, horizontal and diagonal lines.

Upper left: Detail of a forty-sixth anniversary sale newspaper advertise-
ment for Frank Brothers
Upper right: A knotted decorative paper cord. Japanese.
Lower left: A decorative garment *(mola)*. San Blas Indian, Panama.
Lower right: Detail; a video tape package.

37

rier of the visual expression. Line may be thin, wispy, or fragmented in pulsing thick and thin variations. Line may be heavy, dramatic, gushing forth in blobbing spurts. Thick, thin, curved, straight, bumpy, smooth, continuous, intermittent, fluid, and ridged characteristics determine the quality of line. The designer carefully observes the quality of line in the environment and uses line imaginatively as a strong visual element in creating an expanding visual vocabulary.

38

Line is often the first element used by the designer to sketch preliminary, trial ideas.
Upper: Abstract sketch. Artist: George James.
Lower: Sketch of horse. Artist: George James.

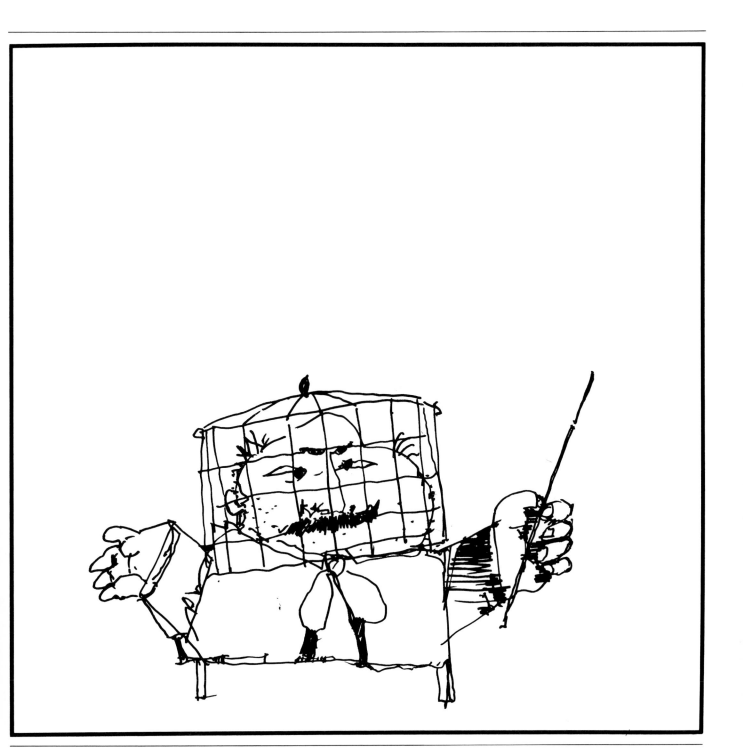

Figure with caged head. Artist: George James.

39

Value — Value refers to the relative lightness or darkness of areas in a design. A study of value is a study of contrasts—opposites put to remarkable use in art, but with fundamental counterparts in nature: day and night, winter and summer, wet and dry. Designers make use of a scale of values (sometimes referred to as tones or shades). How that scale is used depends on the designer's degree of sensitivity in distinguishing and creating more and more gradations. Designers learn to select from an array of intermediate steps from black to white. In the process the eye becomes a finely tuned instrument.

Literally hundreds of gradations are possible depending upon fine control and patience. The Munsell color system, described in the section on color that follows, utilizes a nine-step scale between pure white and darkest black. This value scale forms the central trunk of a three-dimensional color tree with ten major hues arranged in spectral order with each pure hue positioned to match its corresponding neutral gray value. A designer must understand the relation between value and each of the other elements of art: line, color, texture, and shape. Each element must exhibit some value contrast against the ground where it appears in order to maintain visibility.

The designer is concerned with much more than visibility, although controlled degrees of visibility constitute one important function of skilled value handling. Japanese art displays an unusual sensitivity to value and in recognition of its potential a special name emerged—*notan,* literally the art of dark and light composition. The concept of notan does not refer to

40

Upper: A Japanese woodblock print of a carp uses a modulation of
value to describe shape.
Lower: An Indonesian batik leaf pattern is a bold interplay of three
values.

41

The designer makes use of value contrasts often completely free of implied light and shadow sources. This is called *Notan*.
Upper Left: Detail; a wool blanket or robe showing striking use of bold value contrasts. Tlingit, Vancouver Island, Canada, late nineteenth century. Artist: Mary E. Hunt.

light and shadow, such as a light source illuminating a cylindrical object, an egg, or a face. Light and shadow is a Western preoccupation, albeit a legitimate concern in creating the illusion of three dimensionality on a two-dimensional surface. One finds two historical terms in art literature describing various aspects of light and shadow: *chiaroscuro* and *tenebrism,* two techniques dealing with representation of objects and figures in space. Chiaroscuro is careful modulation of value from light to dark describing three-dimensional form. Tenebrism is the use of extreme contrasting chiaroscuro to create highly dramatic, theatrical three-dimensional effects.

In contrast, the art of dark and light deals with creative and often purposeful deploying of dark, medium, and light values in composition, *completely free from implied light sources.* Value contrasts may be subtle and close, gradations may be introduced where needed, or the contrasts may be abrupt. In both figurative and nonfigurative themes, imaginative value is essential in building compositions.

The artwork of many non-Western cultures reveals art forms that ignore or neglect conventional light and shadow altogether. One may learn much from close inspection of such imaginative design. Also, a study of natural forms leads to the discovery of astounding value contrasts and subtleties—the dark/light pattern in a shell, the miraculous feather spotting in the mallard duck, the striking darks and lights of Apaloosa horses and zebras. The visual appeal of these examples does not at all rely on illumination and shadow. It is the wonder of this world of value that should excite the eye of the artist. Understanding and command of value composition brings creative strength to the designer.

Upper right: Detail; a poster design juxtaposing shapes defined by contrasting values.
Lower left: Record album cover with rich diversity of values. Artist: Roy Applebaum.
Lower right: Detail; a kiosk poster, Switzerland, uses value gradations.

43

44

The rainbow, a natural spectrum, is formed by sunlight refracted by rain-drops, dispersed into a continuous band of colors ranging from red through orange, yellow, green, blue, and purple.

Color — Color is the most complex and potentially intoxicating element of the visual vocabulary. The rainbow, arched across the sky, dramatically displays the spectrum hues: red, orange, yellow, green, blue, and purple. The extraordinary variations and unlimited combinations possible with color allow the formation of visual compositions that can express a broad range of human moods and emotions.

The designer studies the physical properties of light and color, human responses to color, and historical symbolism to make visually informed color decisions. Knowledge of color theory gives the designer the skill to mix and change basic hues. The artistic and inspired use of color, however, may well rely on intuitive and subjective feelings. Keep this in mind as the properties of color are examined.

In about 1676, Sir Isaac Newton caused a beam of sunlight to pass through a prism; the ray of white light dispersed into a continuous band of colors ranging from red through orange, yellow, green, blue, to purple. By means of a converging lens he then collected these colored rays, to produce white light again. Each hue can be accurately defined by specifying its wavelength and frequency. The light waves are not actually colored but the hu-

Examples of the six basic hues found in the spectrum.

45

man eye and brain, through a process still not completely understood, can discriminate each wavelength as specific color. Light rays discerned as red, blue, and green are known as additive primary colors. In light, any color can be produced by mixing various quantities of these rays and when all three are mixed together white light results.

The colors of objects result from light absorption and are known as subtractive colors. A green apple looks green because it absorbs all other colors of light and reflects only green. When light is totally absorbed by a surface, the result is black. If opposing colored filters such as red and green are placed before a spotlight, the result will also be black because the red filter absorbs all the rays except green and the green filter absorbs all the rays except red.

Further study of prismatic dispersion of light, the specific frequencies and wavelengths of colored light rays, and the additive properties of colored light is recommended for designers who may wish to work with light in the field of theater staging and environmental design. The designer is most frequently involved with color through the use of pigment and colored materials, however. The following discussion outlines

Upper: A green apple looks green because it absorbs all other colors of light and reflects only green.
Lower: When pigment colors are mixed, a subtractive process produces a wide range of color variations.

Neon light penetrates the dark night sky with
bright and dazzling color.

47

a terminology of color so the designer can communicate with accuracy the specifics of any given color.

Pigment is any colored powdered substance which when mixed with suitable liquids forms paints, dyes, glazes, enamels, etc. Pigment colors are absorptive colors. They are seen as a result of light subtraction. Keep in mind that color mixing in pigment is quite different from color mixing in light. In pigment color the three primaries are red, yellow and blue. If these three primaries are mixed in certain proportions, the subtractive result is neutral or no color.

Color is made up of three distinct visual properties: *hue, value,* and *intensity.*

Hue is the specific name of a color. It is color in its purest form: clear blue, red, green, yellow, purple.

Value is the relative lightness or darkness of a color. Each hue in its pure form has a specific

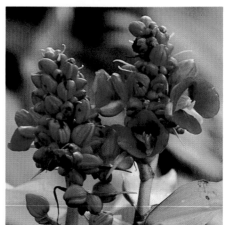

The six basic hues are found in our everyday environments.

value, ranging from very light to very dark. Yellow in its purest form is very light. Blue in its purest form is relatively dark. Each hue may be made lighter by adding white or darker by adding black. A full range of values for each hue results from controlling the amount of black or white added. A very light red is called pink and a very dark red is called maroon.

Intensity is the relative brightness or dullness of a color. Pure hues also vary in their relative intensity: pure red is a relatively bright hue while blue is not quite as bright. In mixing pigments, a hue is made duller by the addition of its complement, the hue opposite on the color circle. Green may be slowly added to red until the redness disappears. If value is imagined as a tree trunk with black at the base moving upward to white at the top, intensity is a horizontal branch with dull next to the trunk, growing brighter as the branch reaches out from the trunk. It should be noted that while white and black primarily alter the value of a hue, the addition of black or white also affects intensity. However, the essential factor in modifying intensity is the addition of the complementary hue.

Color theory based on the properties of hue, value, and intensity have intrigued artists

Upper left: Red orange machinery wheel creates strong value contrast against a dark ground. Intermediate values occur within the wheel form.
Upper right: Strong contrast of value combined with bright color against neutrals.
Middle left: A range of muted shades and delicate tints suggest a quiet softness in this design.
Middle right: Contrasts of intensity and value enliven the neck design of this Guatemalan blouse (*Huipil*).
Lower left: Dull colors of low intensity set the mood in a stitchery by Esther Feldman.
Lower right: Detail of ceramic mural using dull, low intensity color.

throughout history. Three variations of the basic color wheel and the interrelation of hue, value, and intensity are in use today.

The traditional color wheel as formulated by Herbert E. Ives consisted of the combination of primary, secondary, and tertiary hues, a wheel of twelve distinct hues arranged in the natural spectral order from red to red-violet. Red, yellow, and blue constitute the primary hues because they cannot be produced by mixing. A mixture of two primary hues results in secondary hues of green (a mixture of yellow and blue), orange (yellow and red), and violet (red and blue). Tertiary hues result from mixing primary and secondary hues. They are yellow-orange, red-orange, red-violet, blue-violet, blue-green, and yellow-green, thereby completing the range of twelve hues.

The color wheel as devised by Wilhelm Ostwald recognized four basic chromatic color sensations: yellow, red, blue, and sea green. To make the wheel more complete, red was combined with yellow to produce orange, blue and red to produce purple, blue and sea green to form turquoise, and yellow and sea green to form leaf green. Ostwald continued the mixtures to produce one hundred hues, but later reduced the number to twenty-four, a more workable number.

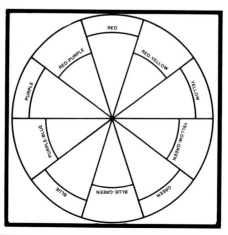

Albert Munsell's color system starts with five basic hues that he believed were, for psychological reasons, unique and separate: red, yellow, green, blue, and purple. Mixing two adjacent hues results in intermediate hues called yellow-red, blue-green, red-purple, purple-blue. A mixture of a basic hue and an intermediate hue results in a second intermediate level of hues with such names as purple red-purple, blue purple-blue, and green yellow-green. Munsell recognized one hundred gradations around the wheel but, for working purposes, a wheel of ten hues was developed.

50

Upper: Diagram of a twelve hue color circle devised by Herbert Ives.
Middle: Diagram of a twenty-four hue color circle formulated by Wilhelm Ostwald.
Lower: Diagram of Albert Munsell's ten hue color circle.

A twelve hue color circle composed of three
primary hues, three secondary hues, and six
tertiary hues.

Color can play a dynamic role in composition. Just as a musician may know the rules of counterpoint and still be a dull composer, the knowledge of color systems does not ensure inspired color composition for the designer. A successful use of color is often related to color combinations that build harmony. This may be accomplished in several ways.

MONOCHROMATIC HARMONY is the use of one hue, varied in value and intensity. Variation can be endless, even in this simplest of all harmonies. A composition of deep, dull reds—somber, rich, and warm—with accents of small bits of intense bright red expresses a harmony in which pure color shines like a jewel in a somber world. A composition of light, powdery clear pinks shifting through a subtle range of slight value variation is yet another solution.

COMPLEMENTARY HARMONY starts with hues opposite each other on the color wheel. These opposites affect each other in a number of ways. Used at full intensity in adjacent areas, they tend to intensify or excite each other. Mixed together, the intensity of each hue is lessened and tones of rich chromatic nuances result. Painters of the Renaissance often used one hue as underpainting and its comple-

Left: Upper, middle, lower: A series of monochromatic harmonies.
Right: Upper, middle, lower: A series of complementary harmonies.

52

Left: Upper, middle, lower: A series of analogous harmonies.
Right: Upper, middle, lower: A series of triad harmonies.

53

Upper left: A linear design makes use of three equidistant hues.
Upper right: The CBS logo in contrasting complementary colors.
Lower left: An analogous color combination of red, red-orange, and orange.
Lower right: A nonfigurative design of monochromatic color.

ment in tinted overpainted varnishes to produce rich, chromatic tones. Impressionists and pointillists often placed pure dots of complementary hues next to each other. When viewed at a distance, an optical mixing takes place in the eye of the viewer.

The phenomenon of after-image, seeing a color after having stared at its opposite, illustrates the physiological necessity for the eye to seek complementary balance. The eye will spontaneously generate the complement if it is not present.

ANALOGOUS HARMONY uses hues adjacent to one another on the color wheel such as blue, blue-purple, and purple. Analogous hues form close, modulated variations that may be extended in value and intensity to encompass a wide range of expressive subtleties.

TRIAD HARMONY is formed from three hues equidistant from each other on the color wheel, such as yellow, blue, and red. As in the other basic harmonies, these hues may be adjusted in value and intensity.

In addition to these four harmonic relationships, color composition may be based on such contrasts as warm/cool, light/dark, bright/dull.

Warm colors are generally thought of as exciting and active. They tend to make objects seem

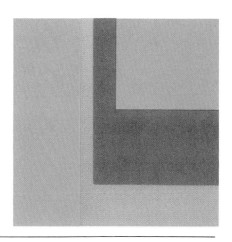

Left: Upper, middle, lower: Three examples of light/dark color combinations.
Right: Upper, middle, lower: Three examples of warm/cool color combinations.

55

closer. Red suggests fire, passion, and sometimes danger. Orange is felt to be the most energetic color and yellow is often associated with light and sun power.

Cool colors are generally thought of as quiet and relaxing. Blue appears in its lightest azure in the upper atmosphere and the deepest blue-black in the night sky. Blue is often used to give a feeling of peace and contentment. Green is also cool and suggestive of plant life and freshness. Purple may be warm or cool and has often been used as a color of splendor and dignity.

Special symbolic color associations are not as important in our contemporary life as in some historic and primitive cultures; however, in our culture, red, white, and blue together indicate special patriotic symbolism. White is worn by brides, orange and black are associated with Halloween, green with St. Patrick's Day, red and green with Christmas.

Extra dimensions of color evolve from personal reactions to individual color and color associations. The rich yellows of early morning change to bleached lightness of midday, and to mellow orange as light fades in the early evening. Seasonal change evokes dramatic associations, generated from thoughts of rust-colored autumn leaves, the frosty

values of winter, April's pale green blades of grass, and the intense hues of summer.

General symbolism, personal experience, and personal likes and dislikes are important for the designer to recognize and control in creating color harmonies.

Upper, middle, lower: Three examples of bright/dull color combinations.

Upper left: An example of warm/cool color in the art work for a postage stamp. English.
Upper right: Mexican yarn design in contrasting light/dark color.
Lower left: A warm/cool and bright/dull color scheme is used in this Art Deco fish design.
Lower right: Contemporary needlepoint in bright/dull color. Designer: Esther Feldman.

57

Shape and Form — Shape may be defined as a closed two-dimensional figure described or delineated by a line or edge. A shape is perceived as a distinct visual unit separated from the ground against which it is seen. One speaks of the shape of a leaf, a penny, a flake of paint. Contour, or edge, is observed and followed. A shadow isolated on an unbroken surface is a shape. Shape may be as simple as circles, triangles, and squares or as complex as the silhouette of a tree, a dog, or a human face. Silhouette cutting enjoyed great popularity in the nineteenth century. The human face was reduced to a flat black shape with distinguishing contours.

Designers scan the environment for arresting shapes, or parts of shapes, and often invent their own. At times the spaces between shapes provide intriguing shapes, often called *negative* shapes. A chief source of imaginative interest is the visual impact the designer achieves in translating a complicated object, such as a motorcycle, into a designed series of flat shapes. The characteristic contours are omitted, producing a striking design quality of power and clarity.

A clear, well-defined shape may generate a universal appeal and become a lasting symbol—a cross, a fish, a key. The designer

A series of silhouette shapes — identification is readily revealed by each contour.

Shape and form combined.
The artist M.C. Escher moves from a distinct bird shape through a transition in which the negative space gradually becomes the shape of a fish. Detail and modeling of upper birds and lower fish suggest three-dimensional form.

59

works with all kinds of shapes and develops a growing sensitivity to their creation and arrangement. An awareness of the power of shape may be developed by working with squares of black, gray, or white. A sense of balance, position, alignment, and movement may be gained by deploying the squares against a white or gray ground and noting the energy, attraction, and weight as the simple units are shifted, aligned, and grouped. Responsiveness to the dynamic visual forces of shapes helps one to place each for maximum effectiveness instead of casually putting shapes on a surface.

Form is shape translated into three-dimensional volume. A circle is a shape; the related form is a sphere. Artists preceding the twentieth century analyzed three-dimensional form and concluded that there are five fundamental forms: the sphere, cube, cylinder, cone, and pyramid. Everything we see may be related to one or more of these fundamental forms. The five fundamental forms are solid, closed entities that exhibit weight and mass. Space surrounds these forms, but does not penetrate their surfaces. While the purity of these fundamental forms is valued, designers do not hesitate to alter them to achieve unique combinations. In addition, the designer may allow space to

flow into a form as well as around it. To create an interplay of solid and void is an intriguing challenge of three dimensional design.

Both shape and form have many other meanings; in addition, they are often used interchangeably in discussions of art. Therefore, some ambiguity surrounds their use. For example, one may read "the artist shapes his material" referring to the act of organizing a coherent, well-defined image. Form may describe the same thing. Each usage refers to the effort as well as the result of the artist's ability to create a unified visual composition. Frequent use of these two terms as verbs and as adjectives may be noted. Form is used in a larger, broader sense more often than shape. Still another shade of meaning occurs when one reads of an art form, referring to dance, mime, pottery, weaving, graphic design and so on.

Form in its larger sense refers to the completed artwork: a successful interweaving of all visual components, theme, mood, technique, function, structure, and organization. All interrelationships are attended to in such a way that the designer is a form builder using lines, values, shapes, colors, and textures. These elements are balanced, organized, and integrated through the use of histor-

ical guides or principles: fine proportion, rhythm, repetition, opposition, transition, and subordination. The designer creates unity when all parts of an image merge into a coherent harmonious whole.

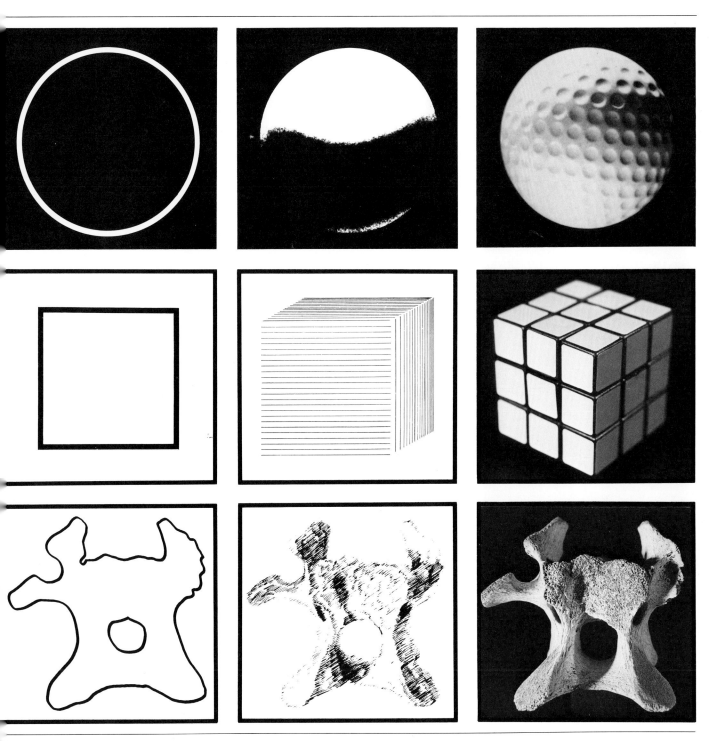

Upper: Transition from circle shape to three dimensional golfball.
Middle: Transition from square shape to three dimensional puzzle cube.
Lower: Transition from free shape to three dimensional bone.

61

An array of Japanese wood combs displays subtle variations of shape.

62

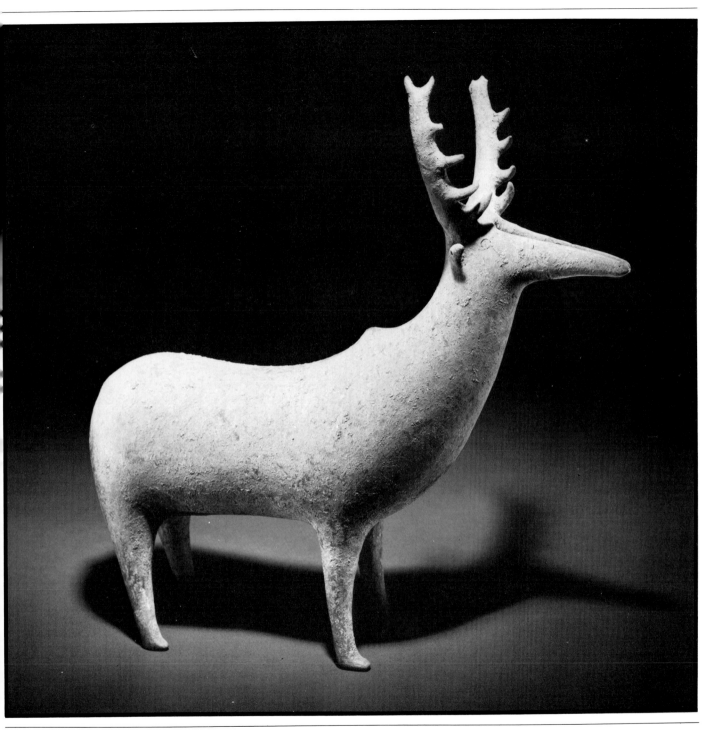

This ceramic deer shows suave handling of form. Iran, circa 1200 B.C.

63

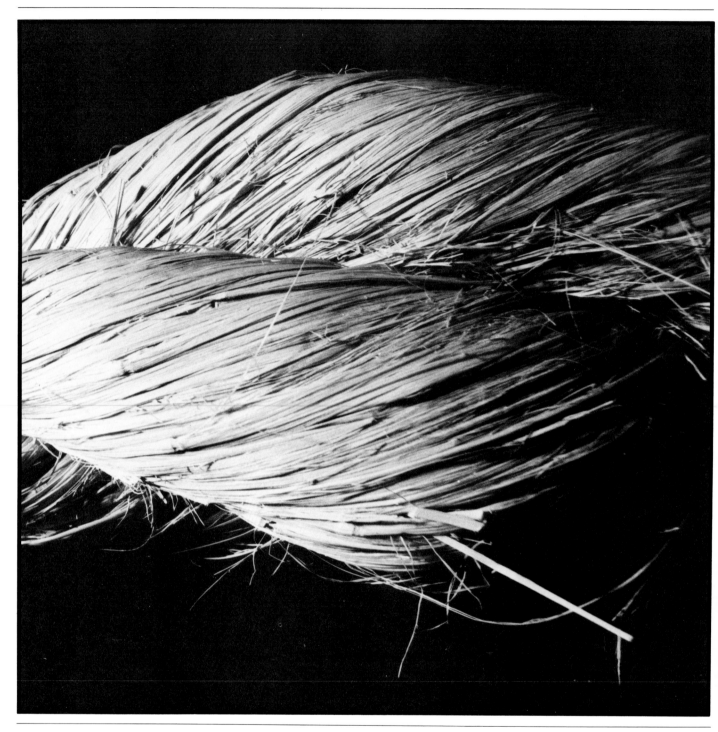

64

Texture is revealed at the surface of a material. Here the fiberous composition of twisted rope creates a brittle, crisp appearance. Japanese New Year decoration.

Texture — Texture refers to the surface of any object, natural or manufactured. Surface texture reveals what an object is made of. Texture is everywhere and adds richness to visual experience. Surfaces may range from smooth, highly polished to irregular and coarse. In the first instance one calls the texture shiny; in the second, pitted and rough.

Texture may be perceived in two different but closely related ways: tactile and visual. Tactile sensing occurs through touch. We feel fur, a soft cashmere sweater, a silver spoon, a mother's cheek, the coarse, irregular grains of oatmeal in the mouth, a smooth custard, celery, crackers. These sensations are stored and remembered, reminding us of what something feels like whenever our eyes come upon it.

The visual response to texture is keyed to the way a material reflects or absorbs light. A polished surface has all the irregularities smoothed out and reflects a great deal of light. In contrast, a matte surface is nonreflective. These opposites describe reflective range, but only hint at textural richness. In nature, visual textures abound; no two leaves are identical, nor are pebbles, petals, sandy beaches, clouds, feathers, etc. Designer-made textures provide the eye with still another inexhaustible source, e.g., silk, satin, wool, cement, plaster, steel, plastics, and papers. Weathering action modifies surfaces and often creates unexpected textures in rusting metals, flaking paint, peeling paper, and bleached fibers.

Close inspection of surfaces reveals rich and intimate textural passages. Not to be overlooked is the textural effect of the aggregate

The polished surface of this forged silver pitcher is highly reflective, creating a shiny texture. Designer/craftsman: Al Ching.

65

sum of individual units, e.g. a mass of leaves, a field of grain, or overlapping footprints at the beach.

Ancient, primitive, and folk arts vividly demonstrate a pervasive love of texture. The use of grasses, mud, feathers, fur, and dentalia have enriched religious and symbolic images. In other cultures, gold, gilt, glass, enamel, and polished surfaces conveyed textural splendor. Today synthetic materials are ubiquitous, but there remains an affinity for natural textures. Many contemporary designers and artists often feature strong tactile effects in the media of ceramics, jewelry, and weaving.

The designer uses implied and actual texture for visual enrichment. A two-dimensional design may come alive with surface variety. The texture of a line may be fuzzy, crisp, or broken and, of course, the implement used imparts a distinctive character. Such materials as chalk, ink, charcoal, and paint vary the texture. In addition, the designer develops a sensitivity to different papers ranging from rough rag content watercolor paper to smooth cold-press illustration board. Thus medium and ground are exploited for textural potential. At times the designer may deliberately emphasize texture while subordinating other elements. Three main approaches to creative use of texture may be set forth:

1. SIMULATED: a careful rendering of real textures such as a faithful copy of wood grain, leather, or stone.
2. ACTUAL: a collage of found materials, such as foil, hair, sand and feathers.
3. INVENTED: pure invention with brush,

Upper: Detail; a pitted, cracked surface of a Raku platter. Designer/craftsman: Paul Soldner.
Lower: A coarse, fuzzy fiber hanging. Weaver: Julie Connell.

"*I like it. I really do. It combines a masculine feel of medieval strength with a delightful sense of play in the portcullis treatment.*"

This cartoon by Don Reilly offers a humorous design judgment, and at the same time makes skillful use of both simulated texture and playful pattern. © 1978 The New Yorker Magazine, Inc.

67

pen, glue, wax crayon, or other tools and media.

It is important for the design student to learn to distinguish between texture and pattern—a distinction often ignored or misunderstood. Texture is comprised of distinctive surface variations reflecting light in a way that conveys a tactile impression. A structure is visible—an orderly distribution of surface irregularities. Close examination of a slice of bread reveals a variety of air pockets held together by surrounding dough. One is observing textural components in a characteristic array. Pattern is an orderly recurrence of motif grouped and repeated in rhythmic progression. Imagine the hexagonal wax compartments in a honeycomb; the regularly repeated motif forms a distinct pattern. Both texture and pattern contribute to design richness.

The designer is ever alert to the textural banquet laid out in the visual environment; texture is useful in enriching design surfaces, stimulating tactile awareness, and enhancing emotional response.

Upper: The designer can invent texture, such as this stippled ink surface.
Lower: Here a varied repeat of one motif, a heart shape, creates a lively pattern.

Space — Space is the boundless expanse within which all things are contained. It is distance, area, room for something as in a parking space. In the visual arts, space can be thought of as both two- and three-dimensional. In fact, the visual arts are sometimes called "space arts" to indicate that the artist places and arranges images in space that ranges from the blank surface of a piece of paper to the unlimited extent of the outdoors.

Space is not considered a basic design element, but rather an exceedingly elastic environment ready to receive line, shape, form, value, color, and texture. The designer usually works on a two-dimensional spatial field that has height and width. Images created on this field may occupy just the surface space or, through the use of such techniques as overlapping, variations in size, placement, and linear and aerial perspective, the illusion of deeper space may be created. In either case, the effective use of space should be a primary consideration.

The area occupied by shapes is called *positive space;* the area between shapes is called *negative space.* The concept of spacing may be clarified by imagining an empty rectangle of paper on which is placed one shape, a circle. Immediately space relations between the circle and all the edges of the rectangle must be considered. Innumerable possibilities exist for this simple placement. If a second circle is introduced the spacing interrelationships multiply. Now the designer must consider circle to circle relationships as well as placement in the area. Spacing must be guided by a keen awareness of size and shape of positive and

Upper: A patch of empty space is visually nothing —
Lower: Until something is placed in it.

70

An abstract figure (upper left) is successively fragmented as the discs rotate creating entirely new positive/negative space relationships.

negative space. Both must be designed, not casually left to chance. For the designer, the central challenge is how the space is used.

The illusion of space is achieved by using various visual cues —
Upper: Such as the use of overlapping figures to suggest shallow space, as seen in an NFL Detroit Lions team poster by Chuck Ren, and —
Lower: By using linear perspective and receding size relationships to indicate deep space, as seen in this illustration by Milton Glaser.

72

The term "proportion" refers to relationships of sizes and shapes within one image, or between a configuration of images.
Exquisite refinement of the relationship of the visual parts to the whole is evident in the proportions visible in the ordered interior of a traditional Japanese house. The size and shape relationships of the many rectangles and the whole interior space are a study in proportion.

Chapter 5

The Image: Interaction and Order

A single visual element in a defined space operates in that space as an independent force. The introduction of a second visual element sets up an interaction between the two elements and the defined space. Awareness and control of the interaction is the primary task of the designer. To achieve aesthetic order, the designer considers a number of visual conditions that are gradually made a part of orderly interaction.

Proportion — Proportion in art refers to relative visual ratios within one image, or between a configuration of images. Carefully considered adjustments are made of visual parts to the visual whole: size to size, shape to shape, line to line, color to color, with all the foregoing related aesthetically to the size of the design field. Aesthetic proportions display a subtle variety of sizes, progressions in space, and sensitive internal relationships of all the visual elements. Intervals, lengths, bulk, contours, and color relations are carefully determined to develop visual interest; that which sticks out is eliminated or changed to a compatible proportion to build unity.

The essential roots of proportion may be observed in organic forms: the sizes and arrangement of parts in the human figure, shells, leaves, snowflakes, blossoms, tree branches, bamboo shoots, etc. Nature provides the strongest clues to understanding the function of proportion in art. Close examination of size and interval relationships reveal repetition within a given natural form; yet there are variations that fascinate.

73

Beauty of proportion and rhythmic recurrence are revealed as inevitable records of the surge and ebb of growth. Such organic unity is deeply rooted in our consciousness, and natural examples teach us the significance of proportion in all design, whether structural/functional or expressive.

The balanced symmetry of the human body provided ideal ratios, analyzed and incorporated in classic Greek art. The Greeks' constant search for right proportions is reflected in their architecture, sculpture, and design—all of which express an order, balance, and harmony that produce a formal stability. The size of the human figure also influences our judgment about everything we see—doorways, ceiling heights, buildings, trees, tables, chairs. We make daily visual calculations of sizes, dimensions, and proportions in terms of the human figure. Whether consciously or unconsciously, relationships of head size to body height, distance from foot to knee, knee to hip, waist to shoulder, length of hands, feet, exert a strong influence upon our concept of proportion. The designer builds on and refines this innate ratio judgment, and brings every visual decision under intense scrutiny.

Human beings have been keenly interested in organic proportions. Mathematicians have expressed in numerical ratios some of the underlying structural relationships discovered in natural forms. Such equations are highly interesting and often instructive, yet to the imaginative mind of the artist the sense of formula dampens enthusiasm as the creative impulse must remain free to invent fresh new proportions. Historically, the Greek geometric plan called the *golden mean* attempted to set up a rule or canon of perfect proportion. It provided a formula of uneven ratios believed to be more interesting than even ones. As a formula, there is nothing remarkable about it beyond its recognition that a space or line divided in half results in a boring proportion. Intervals of thirds are equally dull, and so on. The significance of proportion for the designer is alertness to diversity and uneven interval.

A twentieth-century designer might ultimately arrive at the classic ideal of proportion, but the solution must emerge from intuitive feeling, not from formulae. The designer remains in charge creatively while choosing from an array of possible relationships. The principle of proportion contributes a positive selective energy that enables the designer to make educated choices from the many ideas that occur. If size and amount relationships are too similar, the resulting proportions become static and pedestrian, causing eye fatigue and boredom. Such an unfortunate state of affairs may develop, and if a student designer is somehow unaware of the efficacy of proportion, he or she may be vaguely uneasy and dissatisfied with the offending work. The principle of proportion provides analytical strategies that often turn a troublesome design into an arresting and vital expression.

The designer is constantly faced with making visual decisions about proportion; the decisions may be largely intuitive, or quite logically reached—or a mix of the two mental processes. If the decision is dominantly intellectual, the design product may exhibit a slightly stiff formality; yet a totally intuitive approach may display a loose, unstructured appearance. Balance between feeling and thought is desirable and often more productive of genuinely fine proportion.

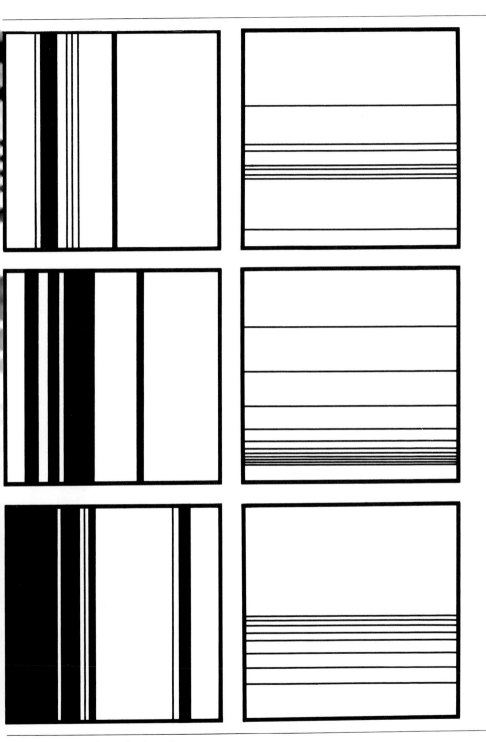

A series of geometric studies based on varying thickness of lines, as well as variety of intervals between lines.

75

Emphasis — Emphasis in design is the creation of visual importance through use of selective stress. A passage is differentiated from its surroundings to enhance attraction and interest. The artist determines relative importance by moving the eye through a composition, pausing, and moving on again. Movement, balance, pattern, proportion, and rhythm all contribute to the unity and interest of design, but the mere presence of these forces may create visual hash unless emphasis is used to help the eye sort out and pause on significant passages. Often emphasis is achieved through judicious use of contrast: a long line and shorter ones, a sudden dark shape near softer values, coarse texture near smooth, an intricate shape surrounded by extremely simple ones, or a circle in a field of squares. Incongruity calls attention to itself. In color, emphasis may be achieved by introducing a very bright intensity against duller mixtures. Contrast of hue may create a strong vibrating color stress such as bright, clear oranges against cool, receding blues.

Without emphasis, the contrasts that differentiate shape and form cannot be perceived. When a visual field is an unrelieved constant, one distinguishes nothing more than a sensation of light and empty space. When differences are introduced, parts of the visual field emerge, generating visibility. Until there is emphasis, there will be no shape, no form.

Since the eye tends to dwell on emphasized parts of a design, the designer selects passages, shapes, or lines to be given importance. Varying degrees of emphasis attract and guide the viewer's attention. While heavy-handed use of emphasis can fatigue the viewer's eye, a rich and varied visual field will sustain attraction. Emphasized elements of a design create visual dominance, whereas less contrasting ones are subordinate.

The one incongruous figure exerts a strong attraction in this illustration for Signature Magazine by Seymour Chwast.

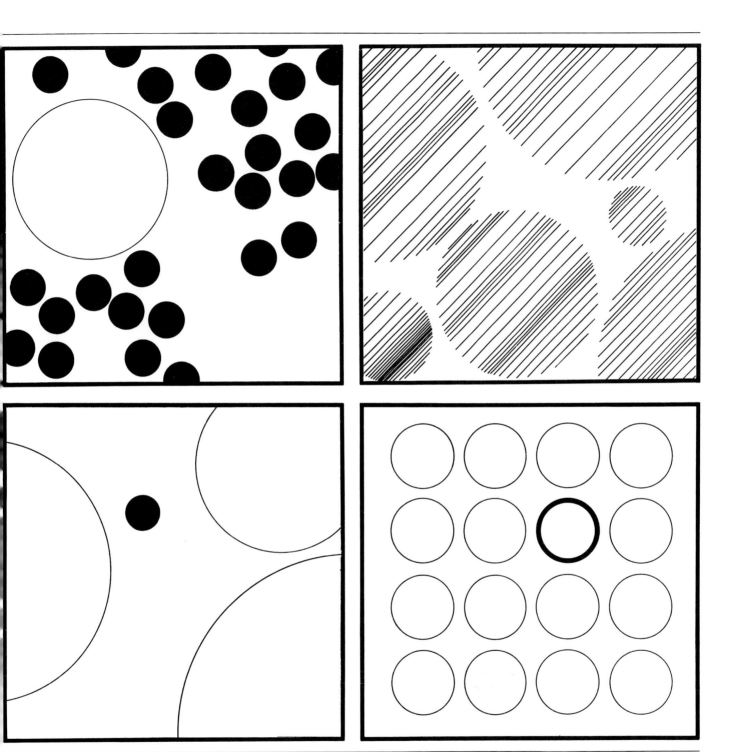

Four geometric studies demonstrate selective emphasis. Upper left: contrasts in size. Upper right: interval. Lower left: dark/light. Lower right: line thickness.

77

Movement — Movement symbolizes vitality, in living organisms and in art. Life is filled with constant patterns of movement and action: running, working, jumping, riding, and breathing. Even at rest, the body elements pulsate assuring continuity of life.

Activities that accentuate movement thus play an important role in everyday life, through actual participation or passive observation. The television screen, for instance, provides endless images in motion: live action, animation, actors' movement, camera movement.

A still image offers the opportunity for a different type of observation. The eye travels across the surface, following visual cues in the same way it moves along each line of print in reading. The designer consciously places images and objects in a composition to facilitate eye movement. Line is perhaps the most effective device in leading the eye along a path. Rhythmic movement may be induced by repeating colors, objects, and shapes. Sequential action may be suggested by slight successive changes in position recording a path or flow of movement. Eye movement may cross the plane of a two-dimensional surface from side to side and from top to bottom, but movement may also penetrate the surface, leading the eye deep into illusionary space through the use of a horizon line, converging lines, size and color relationships. Force or speed lines, fogged outlines, and blurred images suggest a record of swift movement.

Another way to represent movement on a stationary surface is to develop a series of images, each one depicting a portion of the sequential event. The comic strip makes effective use of this technique, and by extending the concept, the animator, using hundreds of still sequential images, photographed frame by frame, creates remarkably authentic action when the final film is projected.

In addition to skillfully moving the eye of the observer, the designer may be called upon to use actual movement. Rotating panels, spinning devices, and other moving elements may be incorporated into attention-arresting displays. The designer also programs the flow of people through three-dimensional space, as in department stores, airports, and exhibitions.

Movement, actual or induced, is a powerful design tool in attracting and holding attention beyond a momentary glance.

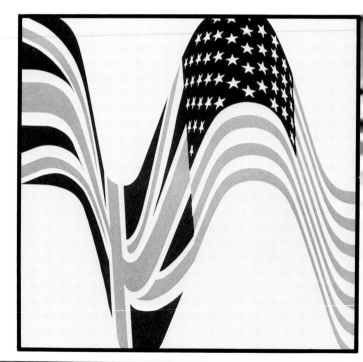

The undulating lines of the British and American flags in a poster design generate an active, rhythmic movement impelling the eye to follow the flow.

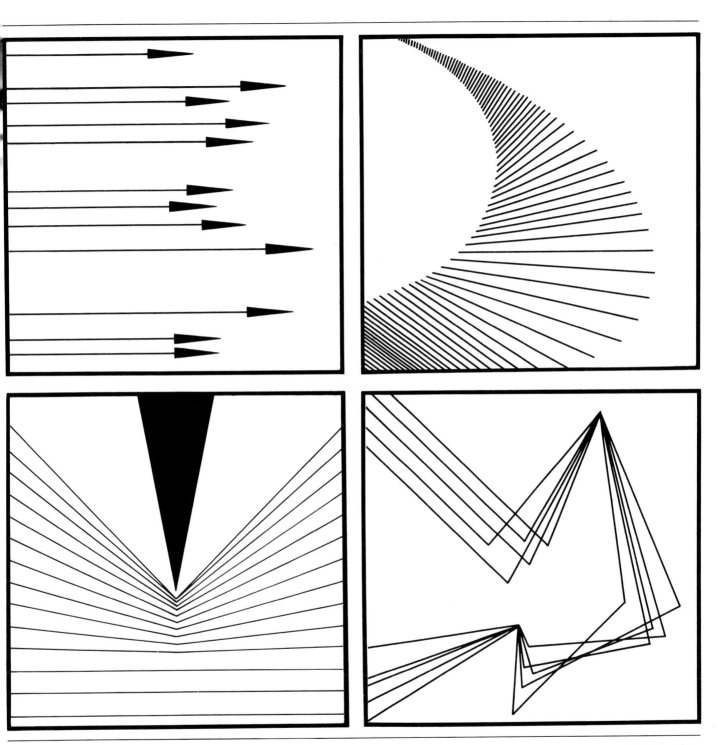

The four line studies above suggest strong movement. An implied force indicates motion.

80

The Dahomey figures illustrate both physical and visual concepts of balance.

Balance — Balance in design is rooted in a fundamental fact of life on this planet earth. Gravity pulls us constantly, night and day, awake or asleep; it is a persistent, felt physical force. The human response to the tug of gravity is a physical effort to maintain equilibrium. Losing one's balance is disturbing and calls for an immediate correction to regain stability. The effort to sustain one's balance is innate; it is second nature to do so and is done almost unconsciously. Balance, then, is an essential aspect of our physical life; it is equally important in art and design.

There are three main types of balance in design: formal or symmetrical; informal or asymmetrical; and radial symmetry. Each is useful.

FORMAL/SYMMETRICAL

Formal balance can be described as a type of equilibrium in which one half of the design is exactly the same as the other half—a mirror image. Many examples can be found in natural forms: flowers, leaves, birds, fish, animals, and the human body. The bilateral symmetry of the body influences many of the articles made for daily use—articles of clothing, chairs, and tables are usually symmetrically balanced. Formal balance often creates a sense of dignity and stateliness. It is useful when the designer wants to suggest poise, formality, and repose. When used with skill, symmetrical balance creates stability and strength. The Parthenon is a classic example of symmetry in architecture.

INFORMAL/ASYMMETRICAL

When the visual weight on each side of a composition is equal, but not identical, informal balance is created. Asymmetry stirs the

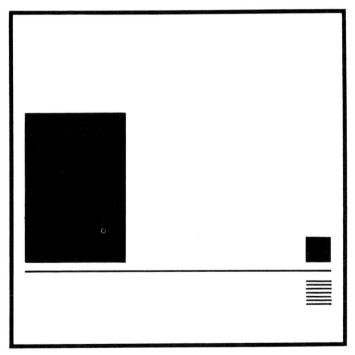

Two geometric studies in visual balance: Upper: symmetrical, Lower: asymmetrical.

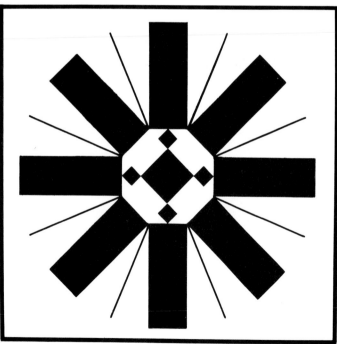

observer, and arouses curiosity as to what makes the design balanced. At once attention is attracted by dynamic, visual relationships. A designer uses informal balance to express action, restlessness, and energy. The range of possibilities for asymmetrical design is infinite.

RADIAL BALANCE

In radial balance, all parts of a design grow outward from a center: the petals of a daisy, a snowflake, certain spider webs, the spokes of a wheel. A classic radial design is the Gothic rose window. All of these examples are fundamentally symmetrical, although the radiating elements create a sense of movement.

A designer can use many devices to achieve balance. A solid shape is visually heavier than an outlined shape; a thick line is heavier than a thin line; a vivid color exerts greater visual weight than a soft pastel. These varying powers may be used to create static, exciting, or disturbing balances. The development of the ability to think in terms of visual energies is a major aspect of design skill. The experimental balancing of visual forces offers exciting design challenges.

Two geometric studies in visual balance: Upper: asymmetrical, lower: radial. Each of the balance examples establishes a sense of equilibrium.

Repetition — Repetition of a chosen visual theme within a composition is used to develop rhythm. Squares are compatible with squares, circles with circles. Recurring shapes, lines, colors, and values create rhythmic linkage. Without planned repetition a chaotic assembly of unrelated elements results in non-design.

In nature, repetition is one of the most striking characteristics of form. It is clearly visible in a shell form, but there are distinct variations in proportion and sequence. Life itself is marked by recurring phenomena: day/night, summer/winter, heartbeats. The arts often integrate and express this persistent life theme.

Composers invent a musical theme, then proceed to repeat it, perhaps inverted, stretched out, played by strings, echoed by horns, or rumbling in the double bass. The theme may be stated briskly or slowly. Designers create themes with visual elements, altering and expanding on the theme in a way similar to the composer's method.

In music and dance, rhythm refers to notes and movements recurring in time. Visual rhythm occurs in space. In design, the simplest example of rhythm might be a recurring series of regularly placed shapes separated by negative voids. This simple example hints at the endless possibilities inherent in the use of repetition. Shapes can be used over and over to build complex rhythmic passages sometimes called pattern.

In design there are five kinds of repetition:
1. Simple regularity—like shapes and intervals, as is seen in a picket fence.
2. Alternation—repetition of two different

Upper: A shell pattern makes use of motif inversion.
Lower: Cotton fabric with a regularly repeated motif creates a rhythmic movement.

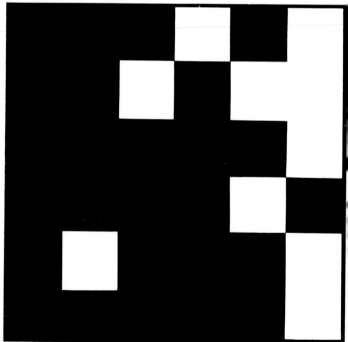

84

Four geometric studies based on recurrence: Upper left: The motif is repeated at regular intervals. Upper right: Two motifs are alternated regularly. Lower left: The dark/light of the motif is inverted. Lower right: A motif recurs at irregular intervals.

elements, such as circle–rectangle, dark–light, big–small.

3. Inversion—repetition in which position of the unit is reversed or turned upside down.

4. Irregular recurrence—a chosen shape or motif reappears at unexpected or irregular intervals and perhaps in varying sizes.

5. Radiation—units fan out from a central point in symmetrical or asymmetrical array, as in a Gothic rose window.

Skill and thought must accompany the use of these guides.

The use of theme and variation creates rhythmic recurrence. Often the stated theme may be disguised so skillfully that the eye is barely aware of the repetition. Aesthetic repetition develops when complex groupings are invented and varied with accent and result in fine proportion.

Upper: A radial design of cut paper. Polish folk art.
Lower: The pine cone is a fine example of recurrence in a natural form. Each cone segment is roughly the same shape, but growth produces subtle variations in size.

85

An arresting design of partially woven fibers illustrates a highly individual interaction between designer and material. Designer/Craftsperson Carol Shaw Sutton.

Part III

The Design Process

The design process is basic problem solving. It is an active dynamic interaction between the designer, the problem at hand, at times a client, the material, and the often elusive solution. The design process is highly individual and difficult to trace from a specific beginning to the finished product. Refinement is a significant phase of the process, but improvisation and redirection may well be equally vital to achieving success.

Process also suggests physical manipulation of materials with busy hands skillfully wielding appropriate tools. Eye-hand coordination and the learning of specific, essential techniques are as necessary to the designer as to the skilled athlete. Manipulation, however, goes beyond physical skill and moves toward expression. Materials are used ingeniously and inventively to ensure an open and receptive approach. A willingness to maintain an attitude of openness characterizes the creative individual. Is the material appropriate? Is the problem clear? Is the communication clear? Is the traditional approach necessary? Who is affected? Is there a better way?

A systematic approach to problem solving is suggested at the end of this section. The framework is structured, to facilitate an orderly approach to a problem, but open enough to allow for personal elaboration.

87

Chapter 6

Response and Expression

A response, whether quietly achieved, loudly assertive or anywhere in between, is a hoped-for outcome of the design process. The design process is a complex endeavor involving inner motivation, attitude, and enterprise —the translating of a perceived problem into a design solution that satisfies both function and individual expression.

Motivation — Motivation refers to an inner drive, impulse, or intention that causes a person to do something, or act in a certain way. In design the fundamental motive is to create something of functional and aesthetic merit. The essential roots of such motivation are difficult to ascertain since the impulse may be generated by both inner and outer forces. Creativity is often set in motion by inner drives, but external stimuli play a major role in stirring inner perceptions. A fine teacher may arouse and help release creative energy by helping to expand the student's visual exposure and by sharing aesthetic perceptions. The work of professional designers suggests a measure of perfection toward which the student may work. A few designers may even take on the role of superhero, setting design trends and influencing others. For the designer, recognition and remuneration provide valuable inducements for designing, but motivation is deeper than just reacting to such external stimuli.

Child art provides compelling evidence of an innate aesthetic motivation—a clear response to an inner impulse manifested in unmistakable expressive vitality. Another motivational ingredient can be discerned in early artistic endeavor: a sense of self-gratification, release, and accomplishment. With maturity, such psychological rewards continue to exert great influence in all artistic endeavors. A new synergy occurs, however, when individual inner energies are strengthened and merged with new perceptions and broader considerations. It is this reaching out that a successful designer must master. Norman Newton, designer and author, provides a useful summary of external conditions that influence the motivations of the conscientious designer.

1. Space and the surface of the earth are two of the most basic working materials of design. THE MOST IMPORTANT MATERIAL OF ALL, HOWEVER, IS PEOPLE.
2. In every problem of design, the most fundamental issue is some human need, some maladjustment or inadequacy between people and their environment that awaits correction.
3. The things and arrangements conceived of by the designer are created as a probable means toward solving some central human difficulty.[9]

Newton clearly stresses the attitude of outreach—looking beyond the self; and, he recognizes that in addition to design other professions, other types of human effort are also engaged in solving central human difficulties. Design offers solutions to visual problems; so, designers attack problems in a way that has distinctive characteristics.

Experienced designers who have analyzed their work have described the demands of the field in three ways. The designer must be an artist, an inventor, and a mechanic. This three-way mix has a marked influence on motivation, extending and complicating the self-actuating forces called into play.

In design, efficiency, economy of means, and physical integrity must be provided; but, a more comprehensive outlook includes a concern for how a completed design looks and feels. The visual considerations raise the potential design solutions above the merely physical. It is the striving for a balance between utilitarian needs and aesthetic qualities that provides sound motivation for the designer.

Finally, attitude toward one's work is linked inseparably with motivation. Attitude affects approach, the actual work, the refinement, and the ultimate design solution, assisting the designer in recognizing human need. Motivation supplies the designer with the energy needed in working toward a resolution.

9 Norman T. Newton, *An Approach to Design*, p. 100.

Expression grows out of the personal, imaginative, unique synthesis of ideas. The expressive sense of the following record album covers is a translation in visual terms of the verbal and musical content of each collection.

Jefferson Starship *Dragon Fly*. Illustrator: Peter Lloyd, © 1974, RCA Records.

Expression — The term *expression,* widely used in all the arts, merits close scrutiny. Basically it describes any outward, visible manifestation of an inward condition, feeling, or mood: a shrug, a frown, a grimace, a smile—physical indications of inner emotional states. In addition to such nonverbal gestures, voice modulation adds expressiveness to verbal communication.

In design, expression refers to the act of overtly communicating a visual idea. The process may be labeled as picturing, shaping, forming, representing, or symbolizing. In speaking or singing, expression may mean communicating in a meaningful and eloquent manner. In design, expression refers to originality, clarity, economy of process, and style. The designer creates a visual solution to a problem, thus imbuing an idea with an individual stamp. In this sense of the word, expression differs from the meaning understood when, for instance, a pianist plays Beethoven. The pianist expressively interprets the notation created by Beethoven—who expressed his feelings and thoughts as he composed. The designer is not the interpreter; he or she is the composer, the creator, saturating visualization with original thinking.

Art students are familiar with the French and German movement called expressionism, a major twentieth-century contribution to the evolution of contemporary art forms. The liberalizing influence of expressionism brought forth intensified use of color and exciting new personal styles of drawing. Freedom and spontaneity were extolled. Yet in reviewing statements of a leading Fauvist, a movement of French expressionist painters of the early twentieth century, one detects an underlying, stabilizing artistic credo. Here are the words of Henri Matisse:

> Expression, to my way of thinking, does not consist of the passion mirrored upon a human face, or betrayed by a violent gesture. The whole arrangement of my picture is expressive. The place occupied by the figures or objects, the empty spaces around them, the proportions—everything plays a part.[10]

It is instructive to note the importance Matisse placed on all visual relationships and their part in expression. Here is a painter whose style was innovative and bold in execution; yet he placed emphasis on visual structure (and design), perceiving clearly the interaction of expression and design. Therefore, it follows, to design is to express. True, the designer is obliged to work within such boundaries as budget, size, and function. Yet expressive solutions may evolve out of those very limitations.

Every designer must cope with translating the verbal parameters of a problem into visual terms. In this sense the designer first acts as an intermediary absorbing perceptively the nature of the problem to be solved. This first reconnoitering and information-gathering step is critical since the success of a design rests upon the designer's ability to grasp crucial elements. Out of this sensitive intake grows expressive individuality. Norman Newton describes design as "clear thinking translated into form and order."[11] Newton amends this statement immediately to include "clear feeling," separated no doubt to emphasize the lat-

10 Susan Langer. *Feeling and Form,* quotes Henri Matisse on p. 83.
11 Norman T. Newton, *An Approach to Design,* p. 32.

ter inclusion. Thus the designer brings two expressive faculties into play. It is between these two contrasting mental processes (thinking and feeling) that one finds the inviting space for expression. Given a set of variables, no two designers will create precisely the same solution.

Three phases are involved in the design process, and each contributes to individual expressiveness:

1. Recognizing and delimiting the visual problems to be solved, and deciding what sort of action is needed.
2. Putting on paper a personal, imaginative, synthesis of ideas as the specific form and arrangement of the concrete physical solution develops. This middle phase, the imaginative, creative one, is the most characteristic phase of the whole design process. It embodies the designer's expression.
3. Finally the design is translated, built, printed, constructed, woven, fabricated by the designer or under the designer's supervision.

Expression embodies a great deal of thought and *work*. Initial ideas are often reworked, extraneous elements that muddy a design are eliminated. As the refinement process moves forward, the designer considers and weighs each visual relationship. *Nothing* is left to chance. The final rendition may express a spontaneous, fresh idiom, but many well-considered artistic decisions lie behind the final design outcome. Expression in design does not refer to a dazzling, spontaneous display of emotion. Rather, it is a quiet blend of thinking and feeling, generating a genuine and meaningful expression.

When designers reach the point in their creative development where considerations of placement, proportion, and empty space occur without conscious effort, their work may be called expressive.

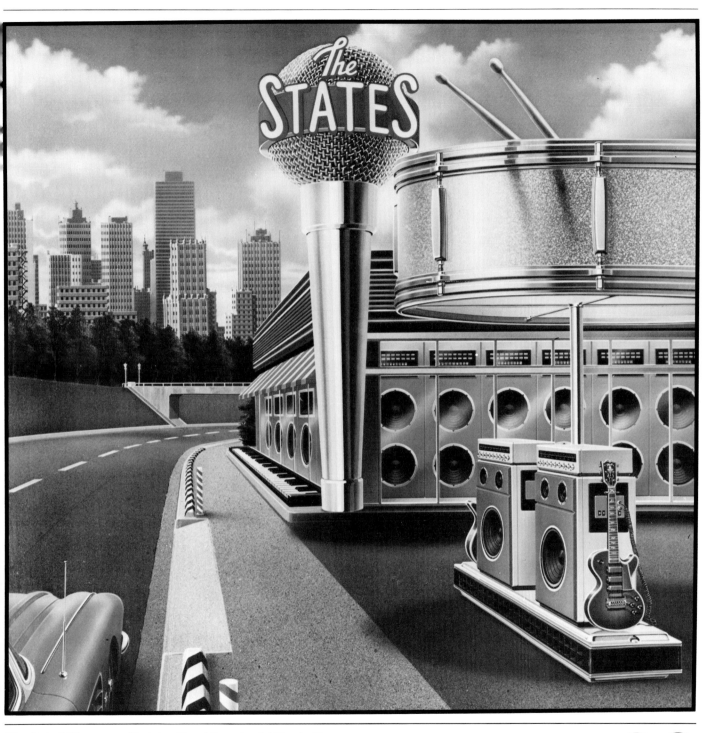

"The States" Album cover-Illustrator: Shusei Nagoaka; Art Director/Designer: Bill Murphy of Rod Dyer, Inc. for Chrysalis Records

93

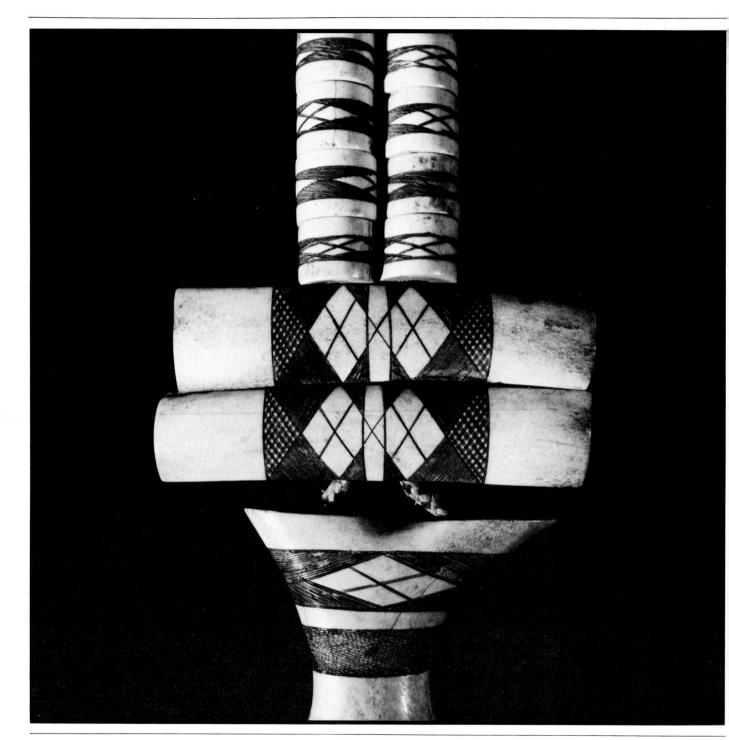

94

A design solution often starts with the selection of an appropriate material.
Bone construction with incised line. Ainu.

Materials — Throughout history natural materials have been used to build shelters, fashion clothing, and make tools and jewelry. Bone, ivory, feathers, fibers, hides, shark's teeth, shells, stones, clay, wood, and bark all have been put to use. Today the designer also has access to many sophisticated synthetics.

A study of materials is essential in the education of a designer. Designers at the Bauhaus, an early twentieth-century design school founded in Germany by Walter Gropius, recognized that it was virtually impossible to separate the knowledge of materials from the design process as the two interact so intimately. The basic course at the Bauhaus reflected this kinship. A material should be chosen to serve efficiently and appropriately. For example, rosewood might be inappropriate for a kitchen counter top where utility and efficiency are called for. Each material presents the designer with possibilities as well as limitations.

All materials possess inherent aesthetic properties. Respect for materials is often called "truth to materials." Wood, for example, is warm in appearance, fibrous in consistency; it can be carved, turned, split, and cut. The density of wood varies a great deal; pine and fir are soft; ironwood and teak are heavy and tough. By rubbing and sanding, the final finish can be made velvety smooth, enhancing the inherent wood grain and soft, warm texture. In contrast, the high gloss of shiny commercial varnishes is foreign to wood, damaging and diminishing its visual integrity. Glass and metal are harder and colder, and provide durable surfaces that range from

Upper: Decorated clay vessel. Acoma, American Indian.
Lower: Organically shaped brass box, India.

95

Upper left: Stone lion's head. English.
Upper right: Leaded glass window. Artist: Steve Samuelson.
Lower left: Bamboo and oiled paper umbrella. Japanese.
Lower right: Detail, Ikat dyed fabric, nineteenth century Arabic.

Upper left: Paper lamp. Japanese.
Upper right: Decorative dough angel. Designer: Dextra Frankel.
Lower left: Decorated clay vessel. Designer: Scott Young.
Lower right: Detail; wood storage unit. Designer: Dextra Frankel.

97

pitted and textured to highly polished. Each can be melted at high temperatures, rolled, stamped, or shaped by the designer, or poured into molds to duplicate an article many times. Plastics are widely used today—simultaneously a boon to the designer and sometimes a curse to the environment. Plastics may be strong, flexible, transparent, translucent, or opaque, and some possess optical properties. Then there are natural materials other than wood that the designer of three-dimensional products may use, among them clay, fiber, stone, and leather. The designer of two-dimensional artwork makes use of papers, fibers, pigments, inks, and dyes. As new materials and processes develop, the designer is obliged to keep abreast of these and to explore the potential offered by innovations.

Materials touch directly on three major topics discussed in this chapter: a designer may be motivated and stimulated directly by a particular material. Materials are expressive, varying from fragile and refined to earthy and coarse. In addition, certain materials are chosen for their inherent physical properties that relate directly to the function of the finished work. Each consideration demands an alert and penetrating vision on the part of the designer.

Function — ''Form follows function'' is probably the most often repeated statement about design. Clearly, it means that the form of an object should be defined by the work it has to do. When examining the artifacts of our daily life, we expect scissors, forks, and weed trimmers to look the way they do because of operating efficiency. In analyzing the functional merit of a design idea, the basic question of efficient operation is essential. The proportions of a chair are immediately related to the sitting position of the human body. Does a chair support the body at specific points with efficiency and comfort? What dictates the height of the seat? How much back support is needed? How should the chair respond to body angle? As each of these design problems is undertaken, basic efficiency is resolved. What is the essential work of a theater poster? Does the poster present the essential bits of information to communicate a clear message?

While operating efficiency is essential to the nature of function, it alone does not reflect the entire scope of concern. The question of the appropriate material as an integral part of function is also essential. A choice of materials is one of the first decisions a designer must make and the design should in part be shaped by the nature of the material chosen. Natural materials such as wood, clay, and fiber have unique characteristics which need to be considered. Metal, plastic, and glass have other specific qualities. The designer formulates solutions that take advantage of the material chosen. The particular properties of clay make it appropriate for dinnerware, for in-

Upper: Contemporary corkscrew — function clearly evident.
Lower: Stainless steel flatware — unadorned utensils.

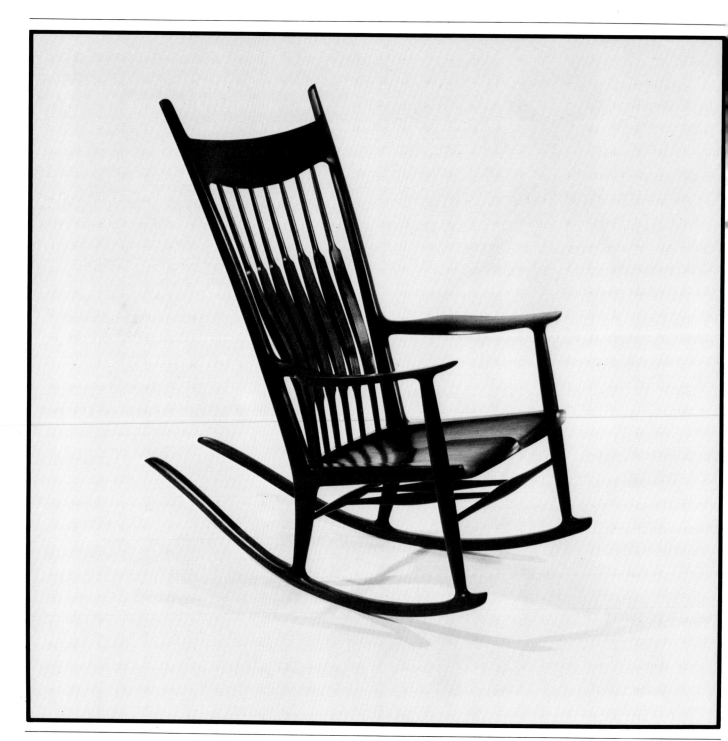

A contemporary rocking chair by Sam Maloof not only rocks and supports a person comfortably, but is a visual delight.

stance, but impractical for use in the construction of a typewriter.

In considering function, the designer also needs to be informed of current technology and processes. No longer hemmed in by the constraints of metal type, alphabet design is now enjoying a renaissance. Push-button dialing, new plastics, and transistorized parts have made changes possible in telephone instrument design. The aware designer constantly seeks out updated developments in the field that stimulate new solutions to problems. Creative design should honestly reflect current technology unlimited by outmoded ideas or redundant imitations of the past.

Function is not limited to physical requirements; a design must also function visually. Have visual qualities been used expressively in completing a design solution? Does the design provide visual satisfaction and pleasure? A dining room chair may not only keep the body close to the table, but may possess such pleasing proportions, sculptured silhouette, and beauty of surface treatment that the pure visual quality may be contemplated. The chair then functions not only as seating, but as an object of visual delight. When these two concepts are harmonized, true function is realized.

In addition to operating efficiency, material integrity, current technology, and visual awareness, the designer should understand that other human complexities impinge on function from time to time. Individual personal needs occasionally play a role in how an object functions. An antique teacup, handed down through the family line, functions as a

102

A contemporary teapot with linear pattern that enhances the frank, functional form.

container for drinking tea, but may also fulfill a need for a link to the past.

The purity suggested by "form follows function" has long been the goal of the designer. As one seeks to meet this ideal, consideration needs to be given to the complexities of function, always loyal to clarity and economy and yet sensitive to the varied range of human needs.

A Berlina coupe — a classic auto design. When parked in the driveway, it functions as ready transportation, but may also serve as an expression of personality and/or economic status.

104

The sun symbol appears throughout history imbued with a variety of meanings ranging from a sacred diety to pure decoration.
Upper left: A printer's emblem from Italy, 1500-1526.
Upper right: Detail from a woodcut by Albrecht Durer, 1498.
Lower left: Identifying mark of the Sun Insurance Co., England, 1711.
Lower right: A contemporary sun symbol. Designer: Kazuo Kuwabara.

Symbolism — Symbols are a systematic combination of sounds, marks, or images used to transfer information or ideas. In visual communications, both word and pictorial symbols are used to convey to the mind an image of something else. The morning newspaper, a concise collection of symbols, spurs us with words and images to think and feel the joy, anxiety, and hope of recent events and also urges us to buy, travel, eat, and otherwise partake of life—and the advertisers' products.

A wide range of visual symbols confronts us daily, each communicating an idea or a message. The visual form of the message may be highly personal, such as the crude spray-can graffiti in the subway, or it may be highly intellectual, such as a refined corporate identity logo on the glass tower in the center of a financial district. In fine art the visual symbol may be so personal that communication is hardly more than an indistinct whisper. In the field of graphic design, the visual symbol is so precise and refined that it not only communicates clearly but also becomes a visual delight.

Persons who wish to communicate must have a knowledge of the system of symbols in order to understand the message. Symbols have been humanity's secret

"Somehow 'partly cloudy' doesn't seem altogether adequate."

105

106

Every four years visual symbols are designed
for the international Olympic Games to com-
municate to participants from many countries.
Upper three: Swimming 1964, 1968, 1972.
Middle three: Sailing 1964, 1968, 1972.
Lower three: Canoeing 1964, 1968, 1972.

code. Scholars have tried to decode the symbols scratched and painted upon the walls of caves in an effort to understand the coded messages left by early human beings. The pictographs of ancient Egypt and the early Christian symbols of medieval Europe are only understood fully by those who have studied and learned the language.

Today, we spend a great amount of time learning word symbols. Much of our early education is spent in learning to read and write. That there are almost 3,000 different language systems presents communication problems between peoples from different parts of the globe. Language barriers have prompted some designers to join in developing more universally understandable picture symbols. Some international agreements have determined the form of basic road signs and certain danger signs relative to medicine and drugs. Every four years, the International Olympic Games give designers the opportunity of developing picture symbols to communicate basic information to thousands of athletes and visitors who speak many different languages.

While education has traditionally placed major emphasis on verbal rather than on the nonverbal forms of communication, the advertising industry learned long ago that the most meaningful communication is predominantly nonverbal. The Smokey Bear symbol is credited by the U.S. Forest Service with preventing thousands of forest fires and millions of dollars in fire loss. Smokey is a symbol for four words: "Be careful with fire". The CBS eye is not only a recognizable corporate sign for CBS, but has become a symbol of television itself. Symbols in advertising do not always remain as constant as these examples. In the 1950s and '60s, the large chromed car was used as a success symbol, while in the late 1970s, a new fuel-efficient, trimmed-down model was presented as the ideal American symbol. In advertising, the symbol must not only communicate, it must also be fresh and appealing.

Propaganda techniques associated with a wide range of political causes also make effective use of symbols to capture the minds and the hearts of potential followers. Posters depicting political leaders, slogans, and watchwords traditionally have been used by nondemocratic systems as rallying symbols. The black swastika emblazoned upon a field of red, a dramatic symbol of power, was theatrically employed by the Nazi forces leading into World War II. The symbol of power turned, for most, into a symbol of fear and terror and even today evokes strong emotional responses.

The atomic mushroom cloud evokes another form of fear and terror. It is an effective symbol for antinuclear groups and is used in current propaganda. Emotionally charged symbols often urge people to action.

Symbols are also an integral part of religion and its expression. Various individual symbols, such as the cross, may take on very different meanings depending on the traditions of a particular religion. To primitive people, the cross was a symbol of solar origin. In Babylon, the cross was associated with water deities; in Assyria, it was an emblem of creative power and eternity; in India, it represented the heavens and immortality. Among the Mayas, it was a sign of rejuvenation, and in Greece a sign of rebirth. The cross of Calvary became the symbol of the crucifixion that changed the course of history by becoming the guidance, inspiration, counsel, and hope for millions of Christians. Today, the visual form of the cross varies to meet the requirements of specific religious traditions.

The visual form of symbols is, to a great extent, affected by the personal expression of the designer. Each object symbolized can be understood or seen in a number of ways by the designer and it is impossible to express simultaneously all the possible meanings inherent in an object. The expression of one meaning may, in fact, obscure or contradict another point of view. Anyone who would create a visual symbol must research and select the essential bits of information, then carefully refine the visual image to convey the essence of an idea. The well-designed symbol is a construction of visual elements that communicate an idea clearly.

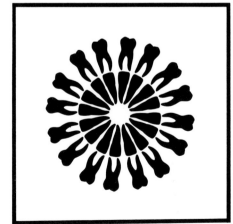

The corporate identity mark becomes an important symbol of modern life. Communication may be broad based, or limited to a specialized audience.
Upper: Left — Minnesota Zoo; Center — Hartford Whalers; Right — Northwest Orient Airlines.

Middle: Left — Fuji Ace Golf Club; Center — Columbia Broadcasting System, Inc.; Right — Marineland Aquarium Products.
Lower: Left — Cliche-Schwitter Engravers; Center — Honsador Lumber firm; Right — Ala-Moana Dental Group.

110

Problem solving sometimes involves combining contrasting images to create a new visual message. Detail of a cover design for an Alaskan bicycle touring guide. Designer: Ron Berry.

Chapter 7

A Strategy for Problem Solving

A strategy for problem solving may incorporate six separate and distinct operations. The time given to each segment, as well as the sequence followed, may vary widely with each designer. A logical plan of problem solving promotes efficiency, however. Aimless daydreaming and poor work habits often operate as avoidance strategies subverting and delaying the process of directing creative energy. The following sequence will assist the designer in effectively working through the design process from inception to completion.

Recognition of the Problem — An understanding of the problem to be solved is absolutely necessary before work can begin. While this statement may sound simplistic, the inherent dangers of not knowing exactly what is to be done lead to almost certain failure. Probing questions at this early stage help bring the problem into focus. Are there specific requirements for size, shape, and color? Is cost a factor? Is the audience for the product limited or open? What materials need to be considered? Are production limitations a concern? Are there any overriding stylistic preferences? Specific details and limitations should be listed and referred to constantly.

Spontaneous Trials — Quick, rough jotting down of first thoughts in visual form (often called thumbnail sketches) is a valuable first step in problem solving. It is important to activate the visualization of thoughts and ideas with a rapid series of trial sketches rather than detailed concentration on a single idea. This process is akin to brainstorming in verbal problem solving in that all ideas that present

Solutions to problems tend not to be bolts of inspiration out of the blue, but are the result of a carefully planned strategy of problem solving. *Poof* Artist: Dana Shore.

themselves should be recorded quickly. One idea sketch may set off a chain of ideas worth pursuing. Tangent ideas also need to be explored. Intense concentration and energy is needed for this phase of problem solving. Beware the idle pencil!

Research — One or more of the most promising initial sketches may require additional information before the idea can be expanded. Careful research at this stage can nourish and enrich the growing concept. The extent of the research depends on the scope and complexity of the problem and may range from looking up historical detail to examining recent technological advances. This is the point where a clip file becomes important. It contains an organized, easy to locate, variety of visual material for quick reference. Further research is time consuming work but often leads to a more developed and original design solution. The function of research is to expand the thought processes; the temptation to imitate must be resisted.

Clarification — Clarification is the critical point when the designer decides which idea to develop. As the selected idea is examined, extraneous and incompatible details are eliminated. Often consultation, with the client or the instructor acting as client, takes place at this stage to assist the designer in moving ahead with the most appropriate and promising direction.

Refinement — Refinement is the essential process of turning the selected idea into a finished visual statement. All of the designer's expertise is called into play in making the critical decisions involving visual relationship, processes, materials, and craftmanship, while carefully preserving the designer's uniqueness of expression. Refinement requires diligent work involving painstaking decisions and intense concentration. The end product reveals the care taken and the quality of judgment exercised.

Resolution — Often a design undergoes a final resolution in limited or mass production. Careful supervision during the production phase will help ensure that the integrity of the idea is maintained. The more the designer understands about the production processes, the more likely it is that the design will retain the intended character.

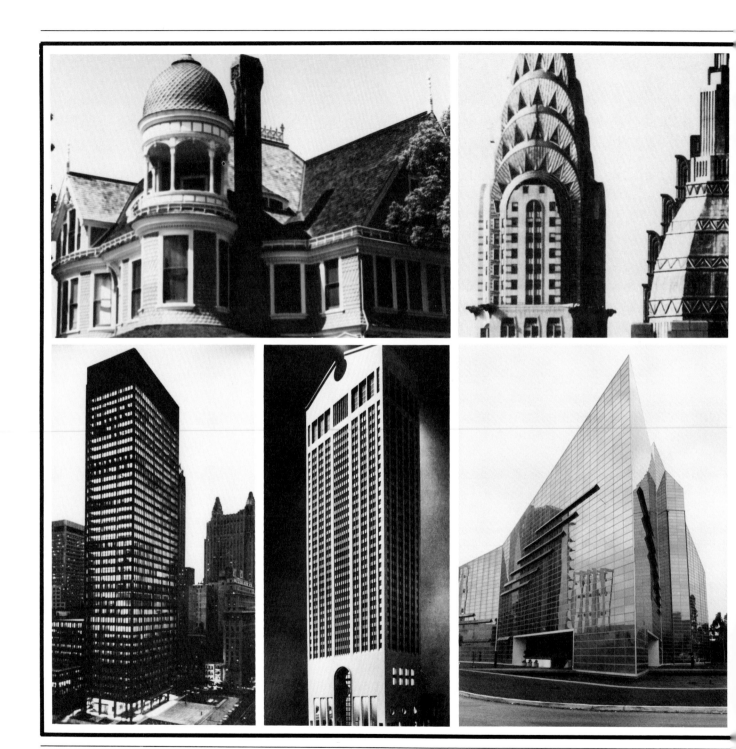

114

Design history reveals dramatic shifts in style.
Upper left: A Victorian residence.
Upper right: The Art Deco Chrysler Building.
Lower left: Mies van der Rohe's Seagram Building.
Lower middle, right: Philip Johnson's AT&T Building and Crystal Cathedral.

Part IV

Design
Influences

The following chapter traces major design movements from nineteenth-century Victorian to the present. Each period prior to World War II exhibits a characteristic look often referred to as style. Design innovators and leaders initiate changes, and soon the new look catches on and becomes the identifying style of a period. Style is the characteristic manner of expression that prevails for a time until an enterprising designer reexamines current design practices and introduces a fresh approach. It is well to remember that style may also mean excellence of expression, and the term is used to communicate admiration in all the arts.

The word fashion is closely related to style; it implies following a popular mode of dress, conduct, and design, and thus has a slightly negative resonance. Fashion is perhaps more transient than style; to many serious designers it appears as a shallow and unstable phenomenon. A designer cannot escape contact with prevailing style and fashion, as all contemporary media take pride in being up to date. Awareness of design developments is advocated, but slavish imitation of a fashionable quirk is to be shunned as it tends to weaken creative vigor.

A knowledge and close acquaintance with historical design movements provides designers with valuable information about their profession. The informed designer tends to function creatively and independently, not becoming entranced with every shallow eddy observed in contemporary tides.

A detail of an early Singer Sewing machine illustrates the Victorian love of decoration applied even to the surface of a functional machine.

Chapter 8

Design in Transition

A full history of design could begin with a survey of the artifacts of prehistoric humans showing how functional objects throughout history have been designed with a sense of visual awareness as well as operational need. Instead, five recent, major movements are briefly described here as significant influences on the design thinking of today. Designers look to the past as well as the present to generate ideas for the future.

Victorian Design — The Victorian period in nineteenth-century history is named after the English Queen Victoria whose long reign (1837–1901) brought prosperity, growth, and rapid industrialization. During this century England consolidated and expanded colonization. Her colonies were a rich source of raw materials shipped to England and transformed by skilled manufacturing processes into products for domestic use as well as for export. The prosperous Victorians developed an intense interest in displaying their affluence in every visual medium: architecture, interiors, furniture, objets d'art, and apparel. A study of the visual arts reveals a preoccupation with showy surfaces encrusted with ornamental pattern, decoration, and an eclectic mixing of historical styles: neo-Greek, neo-Roman, neo-Romanesque, neo-Gothic, neo-Tudor, neo-Baroque, neo-Turkish.

The influence of Victorian style was a worldwide phenomenon; the United States adopted and adapted Victorian ostentation, which spread from the eastern seaboard to the Pacific. Fanciful houses and buildings may be found in every state as Victorian design

118

Pattern, architectural arabesques, and classic pediments are combined in this fanciful Victorian house.

captured the imagination of artists and the public. A vitality was expressed by Victorian builders, although they were blatant borrowers. Vigor and imagination dominated; restraint was unknown and taste was allowed to fall where it might. London was the heartland for Victorian architecture and from that prosperous world capital the influence on design radiated outward. Many nineteenth-century structures proudly displaying Victorian affluence are to be seen in London today.

Queen Victoria's life-style influenced the manners and attitudes of her day. It was an age of sentimentality that overwhelmed much of the design with ornamentation and maudlin subject matter. Results often were ostentatious to the point of vulgarity. A visit to the Albert Memorial in London's Hyde Park vividly shows Victorian design excesses viewed today as bordering on the comic.

Although England, France, and the United States pioneered in the development of modern iron and steel construction, the reigning preoccupation was with surface elaboration. Architectural opportunities often were smothered with historical ornament. The Victorians were particularly fond of Gothic frosting. There was one notable exception to this trend toward embellishment, however.

In 1851 the first International Trade Exposition was held in London, and to house the many displays a remarkable building was erected in Hyde Park. This innovative and highly popular structure was called "The Crystal Palace," a largely glass structure held together by slender iron grids. Indeed, the architect, John Paxton, was a designer of garden greenhouses. He enlarged and elaborated his considerable technical knowledge of greenhouse structure and produced a giant exhibition hall flooded with daylight. Some park trees were enclosed in the design, creating a sense of indoor/outdoor unity.

The impact of Paxton's work was enormous; the unadorned and boldly exposed structure was a vivid departure in Victorian times when ornament tended to hide any hint of structure. The greatest visible influence of the Crystal Palace still may be seen in the construction of several of London's great railroad stations where large vaulting spans were needed to cover the station platforms and many tracks. Three cleanly arching glazed sheds of iron and glass exist in London's Euston Station, St. Pancras Station, and King's Cross Station. Design innovation occurred only in the rear of these stations; facades often were retrogressive in design. For example, in St. Pancras Station and Hotel, where Victorian pretensions took over, the iron structure was concealed behind pseudo-Gothic masonry. Vacillations such as this symbolize the uncertainty of the period.

The jolting contrast between the simple, clear beauty of the Crystal Palace and the articles exhibited inside did not escape the more perceptive British designers. The search for improved design solutions led in two divergent directions. The earliest and most pragmatic movement was initiated by Henry Cole, an influential and energetic man who had helped set in motion the 1851 International Exhibition. In 1849 Cole published a magazine called *Journal of Design and Manufacture*.

119

The title is indicative of his efforts to face and cope with industrial progress. In addition, Cole tried to introduce changes in the education of British designers, but his supposedly reformed curriculum was a resounding failure as it was based on rigidly disciplined drawing rather than design. The establishment of the Victoria and Albert Museum was a direct result of Cole's efforts; its purpose was to exhibit quality crafts from past cultures to influence designers of the day.

The second and more widely known design innovation was the Arts and Crafts Movement led by William Morris. Morris and his many followers were convinced that industrialization had brought with it the total destruction of human purpose and sense of life. Their recommendations encouraged a return to medieval practices where craftworkers fashioned highly individual products. Unlike Cole, the Arts and Crafts advocates were in no way concerned with the reconciliation of art and industry. Art to them came to mean individuality and the search for truth, whether in painting, architecture, or design. The art they envisioned bore little relation to contemporary reality, and many prominent designers grew disillusioned because the products created were confined to an appreciative, affluent elite. Nevertheless, the Arts and Crafts movement was an important part of nineteenth-century ferment, contributing an awareness of design deficiencies and thus fostering the search for design standards.

The Victorian era's divergent efforts to develop a new approach to design stimulated lively debate as to the most effective way to bring needed change. Leading artists agreed that Victorian design had become crudely eclectic, sentimental, and enfeebled by imitation. Enormous challenges confronted designers who seemed to grope for solutions. The basic issue was: What kind of design is appropriate in a growing industrialized society? Closely related to this pressing question was a disturbing awareness that France and Germany had developed viable design practices that were producing better products. English artists began to question British design preparation and the negative attitudes toward rapidly changing manufacturing techniques. Shall the machine be studied and mastered, or shall it be shunned as an essentially negative influence on design? Both positions were vigorously defended by articulate and perceptive critics of the day as they sought to free design from stultifying and academic dead ends. This turbulent Victorian period marked the beginning of a philosophical struggle that culminated in the reforms formulated by twentieth-century "pioneers" of the modern design movement.

Upper left: Victorian pin cushion of bead encrusted velvet is typical of that period's preoccupation with showy surfaces.
Lower left: Late Victorian stamped mail purse with ornate metal clasp.
Upper right: Victorian charcoal-heated iron shows the use of decoration in everyday objects.
Lower Right: The fluid contours of the pitcher and the fancy floral decoration are typical of the Victorian penchant for ornamental flourishes.

The Art Nouveau style is characterized by fluid movement of line seen in these miniature compositions. These decorative letter forms were taken from the pages of *The Studio* and *Art et Décoration*, British and French publications of the period.

Art Nouveau — The design movement known as *Art Nouveau,* the new art, occurred between 1890 and 1905. The central motivation was an effort to free design (and designers) from a persistent and long period of almost slavish reliance on historical forms and motifs. Leading design innovators perceived the lack of vitality in traditional design practices that produced only endless stale revivals. Art Nouveau designers turned to natural forms for ideas: sinuous, climbing vines, leaves, and seed pods. If a flower motif was used, it would be a languorous lily rather than a sunflower. The pervading visual appearance was distinguished by an undulating, rhythmic, linear flow. Some English designers critical of Art Nouveau called it "The Squirm." An unmistakable linear dominance permits quick identification of art produced during this lively period of revolt. Jewelry, glass, metal, graphic design, and architecture all displayed a fluid organic character that captivated designers of the period. Louis Comfort Tiffany, the famous American designer of jewelry, silver, and glass, created highly innovative products in this style. Mr. S. Bing, owner of the shop Maison de l'Art Nouveau in Paris, wrote of Louis Tiffany: "Never, perhaps, has any man carried to greater perfection the art of faithfully rendering nature in her most seductive aspects."

Many of the conspicuous characteristics of Art Nouveau originated in England during the Arts and Crafts movement inspired by William Morris. English designer Arthur Mackmurdo and illustrator Aubrey Beardsley both employed sinuous curves in their work. Yet the movement was first called Art Nouveau by Mr. Bing in his gallery, Maison de l'Art Nouveau. This title seems to prevail although each European country adopted its own name for the growing modern style. The Belgian Henry van de Velde was responsible for the theory of Art Nouveau and for its dissemination throughout Europe. Van de Velde had started his career as a painter, but through William Morris's influence became a designer of furniture, posters, silverware, and glass, and an educator, writer, and architect.

Although Art Nouveau claimed to be the new art of its time, clear historical threads can be found in seven distinct influences:

1. CELTIC ART. The elaborate curvilinear design found in ancient manuscript pages, brooches, and chalices is a prominent influence in Art Nouveau. The Glasgow designers freely adapted Celtic style with its intricate,

tangled, interlacing, coiled spirals.

2. GOTHIC. Art Nouveau artists were intrigued by Gothic ornament, especially late Gothic, which exhibits a keen observation of natural growth: leaf and tendril tracery, flamelike motifs, double ogee arches, and flowing shapes. This ornamentation is referred to as curvilinear Gothic in England and flamboyant in France. The sinuous line appealed to Art Nouveau artists.

3. ROCOCO. Some of the florid, linear characteristics of the eighteenth-century Rococo period may be seen in Art Nouveau. The effort of Rococo artists to make painting a part of the general decor was also a common goal. Flowing space, asymmetrical ornamentation and vigorous use of curves characterized both Rococo and Art Nouveau styles.

4. JAPANESE ART. Art Nouveau exhibits a number of distinct features found in Japanese art: linear rhythms, pattern, asymmetry, stylized organic forms, and an energetic use of space. No doubt the greatest influence on this period was the impact of Japanese art, which in-troduced a completely new aesthetic expression to Europe. James A. Whistler was the first American painter to find inspiration in Japanese art, and to adapt it to his own individual style as early as 1863. In turn, Whistler influenced Aubrey Beardsley, a major Art Nouveau illustrator. Japanese prints, textiles, fans, and lacquerware were collected by many famous artists of this period.

5. EXOTIC ART. Nineteenth-century designers had borrowed from all of Western art; thus they welcomed the new sources beginning to arrive in Europe. Batiks from Java and sculpture from Africa were among the foreign art forms that excited and inspired designers.

6. BLAKE. The English poet and artist William Blake (1757–1827) no doubt exerted an influence on Art Nouveau. Sweeping curves appear in his illustrations and paintings. Mackmurdo, a prominent English designer, was strongly influenced by Blake. Mackmurdo's design displayed all the characteristics of Art Nouveau ten years before the movement gained momentum.

7. NATURE. Seed pods, leaves, twining tendrils, tentacles of undersea creatures—all of these and more were welcomed as motifs by Art Nouveau artists. Languid and exotic hothouse plants held a strong appeal, as did peacocks and swans with their grace and flow of movement.

By 1900 Art Nouveau had become generally accepted; earlier Victorian imitativeness had been successfully challenged. As an art movement it provided an exhilarating feeling of liberation. However, the movement had a relatively short life as everything created required a tremendous amount of individualized designing. This meant that Art Nouveau design was custom-made and could reach only affluent and elite customers. Nevertheless, the artists and designers who participated in discarding old and repressive conventions contributed to a more open artistic climate that would welcome the revolutionary developments soon to come.

Upper left: A decorative comb of the Art Nouveau period.
Upper right: A book plate designed by Ethel Larcombe.
Lower left: An advertisement designed by Georges Lemmen.
Lower right: A shoe of the Art Nouveau period.

125

126

This Art Deco panel on the R.C.A. Building in New York City shows an exotic influence described in geometric terms.

Art Deco — In the broadest terms, Art Deco is a style of design, architecture, and the decorative arts that began in Paris and spread through the Western world from the close of World War I until the beginning of World War II. The name "Art Deco" was first used in an exhibition in Paris in 1925, the Exposition Internationale des Arts Décoratifs et Industriels Modernes.

It was the world of fashion and interior decoration that developed and promoted Art Deco. The concern was primarily with taste and style rather than with practicality and performance. Art Deco was neither for the avant-garde nor for the old wealthy, but for a new affluent middle class. Large spacious houses were exchanged for more conveniently appointed apartments that demanded less care. Modern chic made it imperative that everything in the home reflect taste and style. Kitchens were no longer dark holes in basements staffed by servants, but gleaming and sleekly functional areas of food preparation. Bathrooms were streamlined and outfitted with new labor-saving floor and wall coverings of jazzy designs. Formal dinner parties gave way to cocktail parties and Art Deco cocktail cabinets became an essential social necessity. Deco was above all smart, designed for people who were on the move, breaking away from old traditions.

All eyes turned to Paris for the new look and from 1915 to 1925 Paul Poiret was the undisputed dictator, not only of what women should wear, but also of the decor that should surround the clothes he designed. There was a rapid transition from the flowing tendrils of Art Nouveau to the cleaner and more geometric lines of Art Deco. Art Deco designers borrowed freely so the range of style manifestations took on many moods. Basic inspiration came from the Cubists, the Italian Futurists, African Art, and the new geometric architecture.

Other dramatic influences included the appearance, in 1909, of Diaghilev's Ballets Russes, which brought a new eroticism of color, fabric, and shapes encompassing Turkish, Oriental, and Russian cultures, and the discovery of Tutankhamen's Tomb in 1923, which introduced Egyptian motifs. In addition, each new technological advance was examined not for its practicality, but for its decorative potential. There was no single best solution in Art Deco design, but rather many diverse ways toward achieving fashionable style. Some of the variations included: shipboard style, Hollywood style, picture-palace style, skyscraper style,

This polished chromium hat stand made use of new 1920's materials and exudes a sleek, sophisticated look.

127

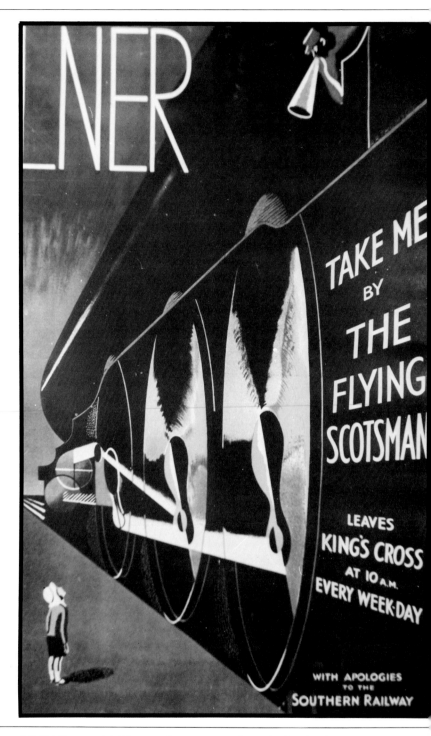

A British Transport Art Deco poster expresses elements of motion borrowed freely from the Italian futurists' love of movement and speed.

nd apartment house style.
Art Deco was a final fling at
andcrafting in which fine materi-
s, rich and exotic finishes,
arved details, and inlaid sur-
ces were combined with skill
nd care. Tapestry enjoyed a re-
val during this period, adding
the enrichment of interior sur-
ces. Persian motifs combined
lashy floral design with vibrant
lors. Furniture designers used
ch materials as amboina, black
ony, inlaid fruitwoods, and
ory while easily absorbing all
e latest Bauhaus material of
bular steel, heavy plate glass,
rome finishes, and aluminum.
acquer was also in vogue and
as used in a wide range of ob-
cts from small cigarette cases
nd compacts to large decorative
creens. Glass was extensively
sed in everything from dining
bles to all-glass bathrooms.
treamlined designs used clear,
ited, and opaque glass with
eel and aluminum structures.
ené Lalique was one of the ex-
aordinary glass designers of
is period. The milky and opal-
scent Lalique glass became a
mbol of the new style. Etched
nd frosted glass and enamel
ith glass were used by other
assmakers of the day. Silver-
niths, ceramists, jewelers, and
ulptors also created a wide
nge of decorative items using
e linear, geometric, and

streamlined charm of Art Deco.
Improved communications
opened up new potentials for
manufactured goods and the
field of advertising became an
important concern. Graphic designers not only worked on posters, the most important form of
graphic communication of the
day, but also on advertisements
in magazines, on wrappers,
labels, booklets and letter head-
ings. London Transport commis-
sioned some of the best posters
of this period. Bon Marché in
Paris and Wesson Oil in America
led the way in innovative advertising design. The fantasy of the
Hollywood musical was carried
over into the design of song al-
bums and sheet music that were
enormously popular. Designs
were bold and decorative type
was an indispensable element.
The richness of Art Deco did
come to an end partly with the
Wall Street crash of 1929 and
certainly with the beginning of
World War II. Many of the crafts
may never again produce objects
of stylish elegance with such
success.

130

The Wassily Tubular Chair by Marcel Breuer is symbolic of the radical departure from traditional seating. The Bauhaus advocated a clean, uncluttered purity expressive of the new industrial technology.

Bauhaus and the Modern Movement — With the advent of manufacturing machinery in the eighteenth century came hopes for great progress. Poverty and material wants were to disappear as productivity increased. Yet, in a little over one generation, industry had begun to disappoint; its early promise had failed to bring about significant improvements in human life. Instead, industrialization brought crowding, blight, and a loss of the importance of the individual worker, who became a mere cog in a giant, relentless machine.

John Ruskin, the English philosopher, became an articulate spokesman against the social evils inherent in the new industrialization. Problems beyond the social evils of the machine were also expressed by concerned designers in England and Europe, who protested against the flow of cheap manufactured imitations of formerly hand-crafted objects.

While the Arts and Crafts movement in England met the dilemma by rejecting the machine in total, the artists, designers, and architects associated with the German design school known as the Bauhaus realized the inevitable impact of industrialization. New materials, new processes, and new technology were an exciting challenge. If there was to be hope for the future, designers needed to control the machine, and the most effective way to achieve this control was through the education of designers.

A new design education was the major goal of the Bauhaus. In 1919 Walter Gropius, an active architect in Berlin and already a proven leader in the new technology, became the director of the Academy of Arts and Crafts in Weimar, Germany. He developed a program of study for designers that would prepare them to meet the challenges of industry and the trades. The name of the school was changed to Bauhaus ("house of building"), and key instructors or "masters" were brought in to develop the new education. In the early years, the plan of instruction was in continuous evolution. Students received rigorous direction, but were also invited to take an active role in the development of curriculum.

Gropius, a strong-willed architect, brought in other dynamic teachers to meet the challenge. Johannes Itten took on the development of the core course. Incorporated in this class was the study of color, form, and texture, as well as the study of the essential qualities of materials. Later, Laszlo Moholy-Nagy and Josef Albers contributed to the

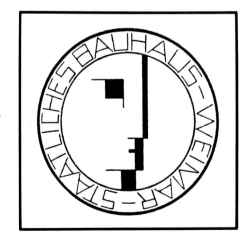

The Bauhaus logo captures the modern twentieth-century spirit of a new design education.

evolution of this central course.

All instruction at the Bauhaus involved both design and craft. The designer was to know the material so well that the expression of the object would flow from structural knowledge and the two would become one. Adaptability to mass production was the ultimate test of the design. There was to be no distinction between the artist and the craftsperson that exalted the artist. Proficiency in craft was essential to achieve excellence. The progressive ideas and method of instruction of the Bauhaus were regarded with suspicion by the academic establishment and voices of criticism were heard.

In 1925 the Bauhaus moved from Weimar into a new facility outside the city of Dessau. The buildings designed by Gropius expressed the uncluttered purity of the new industrial technology. Gropius employed a structural steel skeletal frame, continuous glass walls, and ferroconcrete in creating a design of clean, dramatic dimensions. In these new surroundings the school continued to evolve theory and ideas drawn from a stellar group of instructors, which at one time included Marcel Breuer, Mies van der Rohe, Wassily Kandinsky, Paul Klee, and Lionel Feininger.

Apart from the training in technology and craft, the student learned to express ideas through the language of vision. The Bauhaus carried on extensive studies in proportion, optical illusion, and color. The student learned the basic visual language by developing individual sensitivity and expression. Gropius looked for unique contributions by competent designers, rather than mere imitations of fashionable styles.

The importance of the Bauhaus was, in part, due to its attempt to develop a testing ground for new ideas in art, architecture, and design, and for its innovations in the education of designers. It was a dedicated endeavor to relate a new design approach to the world of technology and craft. In its short life, the school produced tangible results that are in evidence today. The educational books by Kadinsky, Klee, and Moholy-Nagy spread the Bauhaus ideas and greatly influenced the teaching of art. Bauhaus concepts of standardization and prefabrication have influenced a wide range of endeavors. The concept of teamwork, explored and tested at the Bauhaus, continues to be important in solving today's complex design problems. The Bauhaus visual vocabulary, including space, form, color, rhythm, and movement, is the language of today's designer.

A number of products designed and developed during the Bauhaus years are still produced. Two remarkable examples are Marcel Breuer's tubular chair, which uses the quality and structural capabilities of the metal tube, and Mies van der Rohe's Barcelona chair, which takes advantage of the spring characteristic of bent steel legs.

The days of the Bauhaus were limited by political forces at work in Germany. The progressive ideas of the Bauhaus did little to support the strong spirit of nationalism necessary for the development of a powerful totalitarian state. The Bauhaus was forced to close, and many of its teachers eventually found a receptive arena for their ideas in the United States. In 1933 Josef Albers came to Black Mountain College in North Carolina, later to Harvard University, and then to Yale University. Walter Gropius became the head of the graduate school of design at Harvard University in 1937. More than 250 of his students went on to teaching assignments at other universities and schools of design. In 1937 Marcel Breuer joined the faculty at Harvard. Laszlo Moholy-Nagy and Gyorgy Kepes formed the new Bauhaus in Chicago, which continues as

The Eames Home in Santa Monica California is a bold breakthrough in concept and use of new materials in residential design. Charles Eames was a genuine innovator anticipating by many years the principles of "High-Tech" Design.

133

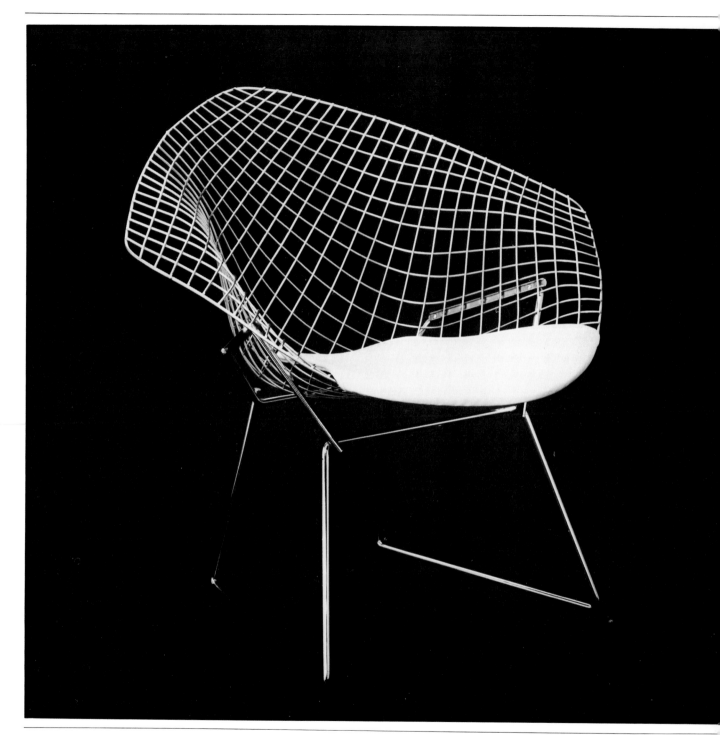

134

A wire chair designed by Harry Bertoia shows an honest and economical use of modern materials and at the same time presents an inviting, undulating look. 1952.

part of the Ilinois Institute of Technology.

The teaching of these influential designers became the basis for the *Modern* movement, which lasted for over fifty years. This pure, clean, and strict design direction, born in the 1920s, was uncontaminated by any reference to past styles. Walter Gropius expressed the idea in a remarkably terse motto: "Art and Technology—A New Unity!" Mies van der Rohe took brevity a step further with his famous statement: "Less is More."

Bauhaus practitioners, in both architecture and design, dominated and molded Modern theory and practice. Mies van der Rohe's move to the United States was pivotal in the spread of the Modern movement in this country. Undoubtedly, Mies's reputation acted like a magnet, attracting architecture students, who in time spread the theories of international architectural design. The leaders of the Modern movement often expressed the attitude that their way was the only true one, and that architecture and design that relied on historical style and decoration should be shunned as decadent—even immoral. The prohibitions were numerous and firm. In addition to insisting on flat roofs only, structure was to be clearly visible with no false fronts to distract the eye. The principle was called "expressed structure." Walls no longer supported parts of buildings; weight-bearing members were steel, concrete, or wood, so walls became thin panes of glass or stucco. It was considered dishonest to make walls look solid or substantial, and color was consistently avoided in favor of white, beige, gray, and black.

The prevailing international style exhibited the designers' strict adherence to right angles, producing a strong geometric effect which ignored organic forms compatible with the human body and its basic needs. It is interesting to note that as early as 1927, Hugo Haring, a German architect, conceived function and form as closely related to what he called "the process of living." Haring recommended designing from the inside to the outside in recognition of the process at work in every organic structure. Thus, his irregular and unique buildings were the antithesis of the strict geometry of Gropius and Mies.

The geometric functionalists, however, won the day on purely economic considerations. Haring's human functionalism simply could not compete with the cool austere rationalism that was cheaper to build. "Less is More" was no doubt an inspiration for Mies and his followers, but too often the phrase became a dictum that eliminated or filtered out human needs for warmth and variety. One critic called the result "impoverished function."

As major corporate structures designed in the spare Modern style began to multiply, cities began to appear monotonously similar. Distinction and uniqueness were rare, and a tiresome uniformity became apparent in the glass boxes that proliferated in city environments. Tom Wolfe calls Sixth Avenue in New York City "Rue de regret" for its unrelieved rows of Mies-like glass boxes towering some fifty stories high.[12]

The longevity of Modern architecture and design can be attributed in part to the energetic promotion of leading architects, art schools, and museums. In 1932, the Museum of Modern Art in New York City decided to advance the cause of Modern architecture by putting on a major show called "Modern Architecture: International Exhibition." The display was organized and assembled by Philip Johnson and Henry R. Hitchcock, Jr., and their book, *The International Style,* was published simultaneously. The book was filled with optimism for the future of Modern architecture. Yet, thirty-four years later, the two authors announced

(12) Wolfe, Tom. *From Bauhaus to Our House*. Toronto. McGraw-Hill Ryerson, Ltd., 1981. Page 4.

135

that the international style had passed.

This was also the postwar period that witnessed a fulfillment of the Bauhaus prediction of the productive interaction of the designer and the machine. The evolution from custom-made design to mass-produced design became a reality. Materials were used primarily for performance and durability. The qualities of laminated plywood, pressed wood, tubular metals, alloys, and an entire series of synthetics such as plastics, urethanes, fiberglass, and resins, provided the designer with an expanded technological vocabulary. The designer's work was also shaped by newly developed human engineering principles. New products were created to be space-saving, collapsible, nesting, folding, modular, and even interchangeable.

Expressing the technological spirit of the postwar period, the work of Charles Eames stands out for its aerodynamic sharpness and clarity of statement. His clean, sure touch can be seen in his house and furniture design. However, in film and exhibition design, the rather cerebral Bauhaus character was modified, warmed, and sometimes rendered playful by Charles and his wife, Ray Eames. They taught designers to perceive with clarity—to collect and store all kinds of artifacts, such as toys, dolls, trains, flowers, old Valentines, bits and pieces of every variety and period, and from all cultures. A warm welcome was accorded to many whimsical, perhaps frivolous, images that might have been scorned by strict advocates of Bauhaus functionalism. The Eames husband-and-wife team exemplified creative openness and a willingness to reach out to all visual sources. A celebration of curiosity and a colorful visual vocabulary enhanced the spirit of their work.

The ferment of the nineteen fifties and sixties in the art world was pronounced and brought the United States to a position of artistic leadership. Designers absorbed and participated in this heady, turbulent period, transforming freedom into design form. The rigid constraints of the Modern movement were broken, and the severely intellectual emphasis of early Bauhaus philosophy gave way to highly individualized inventiveness. New freedom brought new problems to be solved and new challenges to be met.

Upper left: These nesting, white plastic mixing bowls are clean-cut, compact, and visually attractive.
Upper right: This chrome lamp is simple, efficient, and handsome in shape with a polished elegance.

Lower left: A plastic telephone displays an appealing compact form incorporating push button technology.
Lower right: This molded plastic stool exhibits a graceful organic appearance; it is sturdy, simple in construction, and comfortable.

138

Horton Plaza, San Diego, illustrates Post-Modern eclecticism, combining historical and structural elements to create a unique design. Designers: Jon Jerde and Deborah Sussman.

Post-Modern——The term Post-Modern, though rejected by some, is a useful definition broad enough to include a variety of individualistic architectural and design expressions, yet; the term gives credit to its long-lived predecessor, Modern.

Nowhere is the Post-Modern trend seen more clearly than in the major architectural innovations in the new era of freedom from prohibitions. It is not in the nature of artists and designers to tolerate prohibitions; so it was inevitable that a substantial reaction to the Modern movement would eventually occur.

It is paradoxical that Modern architecture flourished for more than fifty years constrained by rigid rules, requiring the use of flat roofs, right angles, and rectangular shapes. Prohibitions included pitched roofs, cornices, and overhanging eaves. A great debate finally surfaced on the merits of the restrictions set forth by the famous architects of the international style.

The search for alternatives was given a decisive verbal boost in the United States by architect Robert Venturi with his book, *Complexity and Contradiction in Architecture,* published in 1966. Instead of strict functionalism, Venturi recommended examining Pop vernacular architecure, i.e., Las Vegas, as a source of new vitality. While he admitted that much of vernacular architecture was commercial schlock, he proposed messy vitality in place of pure, obvious unity.

Post-Modern attempts a change in direction rather than an outright refusal of the Modern movement. The early shifts in attitude

Upper: A stage-set façade is a dominant feature of this Post-Modern house.
Lower: Frank Gehry's Winton guest house juxtaposes several different geometric forms in a playful but carefully balanced design.

139

140

Interior, Crystal Cathedral by Philip Johnson. A steel and glass structure far from the glass-box look encloses an irregular space defined by pattern, light, and intersecting diagonals.

were mild moves toward eclecticism, in which elements of historical architecture were introduced to modify the stiffness of Modern architecture. Post-Modern Classicism describes these efforts quite accurately. Interest in the use of historical forms started in the United States in about 1960 with the major works of Philip Johnson, Minoru Yamasaki, and Edward Stone. In 1961 Johnson wrote of his new attitude toward eclecticism, an unmistakable signal that he planned to practice in two divergent but compatible ways: pure Modern and Modern with variations. He now accepts calling his style classical, traditional, historical, and eclectic—any of these rather than Post-Modern!

The AT&T New York Headquarters Building (1980–83), designed by Johnson and his partner, Burgee, was one of the first high-rise structures to depart from the International or Modern style. The Chairman of AT&T requested that the building avoid the glass-box look and symbolize a new direction in architecture. Instead of glass and glass-curtain walls, the building is sheathed in 13,000 tons of granite, which imparts a sense of solidity and dignity appropriate for a corporate headquarters. The thirty-seven story tower is topped with a broken pediment, the building's most obvious historical form. This architectural head or finial was fiercely attacked by purists who adhered to the flat roof theory. The design revived the building tradition of incorporating a foot, a body, and a head.

Through the years, Philip Johnson has continued to build unique buildings. In 1977–80

Upper: San Juan Capistrano City Library, designed by Michael Graves. A dramatic design utilizing historical reference and high-tech elements.
Lower: Interior of Graves' library. All design elements are controlled by the architect.

141

he designed the Garden Grove Community Church in California. The building is sheathed entirely in glass, hence its popular name "Crystal Cathedral." The plan, however, is not a modern "rectangle" but a complex elongated four-pointed star. The steel girder structure is frankly exposed, yet the effect is light, crystalline, and highly innovative in form, skillfully avoiding the glass-box look.

Another major exponent of Post-Modern Classicism is architect Michael Graves. His design for the Public Service Building in Portland, Oregon, is a primary example of innovative borrowing and mixing of historical forms: Egyptian colonnades, Italian striping, small windows, sturdy masonry, with high-tech and Art Deco features. One critic deemed the building Post-Modern Classicism at its best. The building typifies what Charles Jenks called the most evident characteristic of Post-Modernism: exhibiting "duality and conscious schizophrenia." (13)

Another highly individualistic strain of Post-Modernism is a school of thought that prizes playfulness, wit, and an ephemeral, unfinished appearance. Perhaps this cluster of goals finally realizes the preference declared by Robert Venturi: "messy vitality rather than obvious unity." Often, residential houses reflect the most playful manifestations of this rather radical vein of design.

One architect who has embraced this playful style is Frank Gehry, called "the Maverick Master," the title of an article by Martin Filler in the November 1986 *House and Garden* magazine. Filler described Gehry as "America's most obscure great architect."

Gehry's buildings appear half-built, which disturbs many people. His architecture, mostly single-dwelling homes, is a conscious effort to create buildings which are the exact opposite of what architecture is supposed to be. He prefers to expose rather than to shelter, provoking lively debate by using obviously cheap materials, which he considers compatible with the contemporary world of fast food, throw-aways, and convenient consumables.

Gehry finds satisfaction in funky aesthetics. His own house in Santa Monica, California, is a 1920s bungalow which he wrapped with corrugated metal, surrounded by chain-link fencing. Gehry's neighbors found the result harshly disagreeable visually; it has been reported that a bullet was fired through one of his windows! While this architecture constitutes a rather radical departure, and indeed displays elements of rebellious exhibitionism, it is part of the Post-Modern movement today, making an unmistakable statement that celebrates the "end of prohibition." (14)

In Post-Modern architecture, there is no evidence of regression toward eighteenth- or nineteenth-century Classical construction principles; one sees selected aspects of tradition used to create a lively mix, recalling the past in a vigorous new way. New technologies of construction are retained while Classical details enrich the overall design.

The chief characteristics of Post-Modern architecture are found in its healthy diversity, innovation, invention, eclecticism, and zesty mixture of eccentricities. There is evidence that Post-Modern architects are involved in a

(13) Jencks, Charles: "The Language of Post Modern Architecture" 3rd revision. New York: Rizzoli International Publications, Inc. 1981.
(14) Portoghesi, Paolo. *Postmodern*. New York: Rizzoli International Publications, Inc., 1983.

Post-Modern design often uses playful details that exceed functional needs. Ceramic teapot by Ken Horvath.

continuing search, a steady improvement in the face of criticism of shallowness and a dependence on what some critics call ''package design.'' Post-Modern architects are criticized for being overly interested in designing façades—perhaps a merited judgment. Positively, however, their focus may be seen as an effort to shift attention to matters of composition and visual appeal instead of austerity and chilly intellectualism.

Paul Goldberger is optimistic about the movement, noting: "The best of the new architects are less concerned with style, and much more concerned with such fundamentals as form, proportion, clarity, and common sense." (15)

A return to architecture with special attention to human values seems to be a promising coming stage. It is design minus Modernist prohibitions, design with greater latitude, imagination, and individuality. If Goldberger is correct, it will be architecture brought into balance with attention to fundamentals and form.

Designers were also caught up in the heady, turbulent period of challenge and change signalling a new spirit of freedom and liberated thought. Creativity was directed away from the strict functionalism which had followed the dictates of the Modern movement. The design of furniture, fabric, household accessories, and advertising had been swept along by the vigorous spirit of Modern functionalism in Europe and the United States. The Eames chair (page 176) is a prime example of the spare, clean-lined grace characteristic of the Modern movement, in which color was often neutral with only an occasional primary flash.

This sleek, modern look prevailed unchallenged until the 1960s, when designers and craftspersons working in metal, clay, fiber, wood, and glass began to create in a more liberated idiom. One exuberant counter-style came to be called Pop due to its vivid, flashy colors and bizarre forms. While many serious designers viewed it as garish kitsch, the emergence of Pop was a sign that design was changing and undergoing serious reevaluation. By the 1980s, many designers had begun to experiment with a new spirit of expressive freedom.

Italy's design leadership in the sophisticated Modern style was clearly challenged when a group of successful Modern designers decided to pool their talents to develop a new, distinct, organized departure from the clean modern look. A concerted effort was made to design totally new furniture, lamps, textiles, interiors, and interior accessories.

With the leadership of Ettore Sottsass, a radical design style erupted on the design scene—Memphis. Its name was derived from the ancient Egyptian capital, a Bob Dylan blues lyric, and the home of Elvis Presley. The unlikely relationship of high culture (ancient Egypt) and low culture (Elvis Presley) characterizes Memphis style—a radical mix of elegant high-class materials such as marble, gilt, and precious woods, symbolizing wealth and power, combined with plastic laminates, glitter, and garish colors often associated with cheap design. With obvious glee, Memphis designers scramble and mix these

(15) Goldberger, Paul, *On the Rise*. New York: The New York Times Book Co., Inc., 1983.

A Memphis armchair designed by Nathalie du Pasquier generates a visual electricity with its eccentric and playful forms.

146

Upper left: A glass vase combines both geometric and fluid organic forms. Glass artist: Paul Counts.
Upper Right: An electronic clock in a toy-like structure, a product of Memphis designer Nathalie du Pasquier.
Lower left: A metal chair combining both historical and high-tech decorative elements.
Lower right: Plastic goblets combine a witty interplay of pure cones, twisted stems, and bumpy bases.

ymbols, creating contradictory cultural meanings and connections. Vivid color and playful, unexpected shapes may express both positive jubilation and a negative pessimism, elements both present in our stimulating hurried and unstable environment.

Memphis challenged outright many of the prevailing functional style ideas that had become highly commercialized, mass-produced, and adopted with zeal by big corporations. Sottsass turned his attention to ways of creating design that would be more appealing, more individualistic, and closer to the human spirit. He saw Memphis design as an attempt to cope with conflicting aspects in a complex world and asked why enduring design is better than disappearing design. No doubt this query lies behind his hope that Memphis design will last no longer than five or ten years at most. Perhaps Memphis is little more than surface flash with a trendiness that will quickly pall. Still, its unorthodox colors and eccentric forms have gained a great deal of attention in the design world.

From November 1984 to April 1986, a Memphis retrospective collection toured eight cities in the United States. Some critics found the shapes and colors confused and unbalanced—for example, three unmatched legs on a desk lacquered in orange, violet, and green. Yet, once the initial shock was over, a great deal of acceptance occurred in the United States and even in England. Stephen Astley, of the Department of Furniture and Design at London's Victoria and Albert Museum, has commented, "It gave everything a bit of a kick; it shook things." (16)

Students of design will perceive two similar earlier design movements as close relatives and prophetic predecessors of Memphis. The first was Art Deco (1925–39) with its exotic color, angular and geometric shapes combining inlaid woods, lacquer and stainless steel in richly patterned design. The second, a later and closer relative, Pop art and Pop design, employed audacious color and familiar forms often exaggerated in size and used in a different context.

It is clear that the Memphis design movement has exerted a distinct influence in many parts of the world. A liberating effect has occurred and the spirit has seeped into furniture, dinnerware, textiles, ceramics, decorative accessories, advertising, and fashion design.

In addition to the unmistakable eccentricity of Memphis, there is other substantial progressive design going on, minus any dramatic fanfare. Major commercial design firms feature attractive new lines of furniture, fabrics, lighting, and numerous accessories all of which display the imagination and skill of qualified designers.

In a close examination of *American Crafts* by K. Pearson, published in 1983, one can find an extraordinary range of expressions. This collection represents designer craftspersons who work in many parts of the United States, who reflect a marked diversity in attitude. This collection reveals a healthy state of affairs: it is Post-Modern design with wit, innovation, and eccentricity, as well as with unmistakable vigor and traditional discipline.

(16) Claire Wilson, "Advertising Age," June 2, 1986, pp. 54, 55.

148

A silver fruit bowl, an expressively elegant statement by a designer who seeks to individualize the design product. Artist: Ettore Sottsass.

Chapter 9

Design Innovators

Included here, spanning a period from 1830 to the present, are brief summaries of thirty-five designers. These artists will serve as an introduction to a rich and varied history for today's design student, representing a broad range of ideas and disciplines.

The designers selected are not presented as a definitive list of those who have contributed to our design heritage. Included are major design figures whose names are famous because of their innovative contributions. It is of interest to learn of the purposeful drive and devotion these artists displayed in solving design problems in a fresh way. Each designer chose to channel abundant imaginative energy toward the creation of something that met human needs, both aesthetic and functional. It is this unique perception of the role of design that distinguishes each of these innovators.

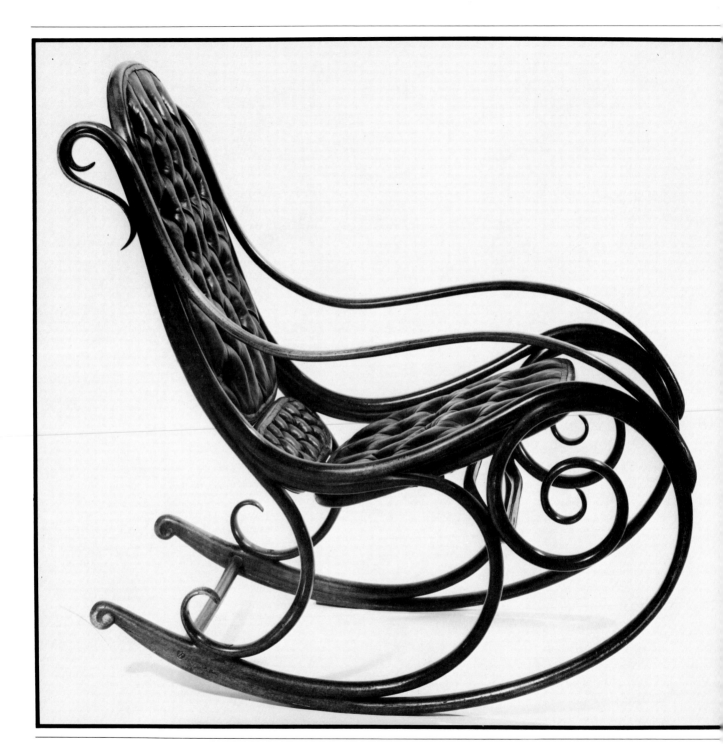

150

The classic Thonet rocking chair of bent beachwood, upholstered in black leather.

MICHAEL THONET
1796–1871 GERMANY
SELECTED ACHIEVEMENTS

In 1830 a young German cabinet-maker named Michael Thonet began experimenting with furniture made by bending wood that had been steamed into a pliable state. Thonet then became a pioneer in the design of light furniture produced in quantity.

Unable to find financial backing in Germany, Thonet settled in Vienna. There, between 1836 and 1840, the steaming process was perfected so that lengths of beechwood could be rendered pliable enough to be bent to form long curved rods. Light and trim furniture was created by combining segments of the curved rods. Thonet and his sons eventually produced *Bentwood* furniture in quantity, becoming innovators in the mass production of a graceful, inexpensive line. The Thonet company developed a well-deserved international reputation for its economical, rhythmic, functional design.

The first known Thonet catalogue was issued in 1859, illustrating twenty-six furniture design items including tables, chairs, and settees. Included in this broadsheet was Chair No. 14, which became Thonet's largest selling and most famous chair. (It sold for $3.00 at the time.) The most important design after Thonet's death in 1871 was the revision of Chair No. 14, newly named Chair No. 18, which incorporated improved stability. This chair became known as the Vienna Cafe Chair, the largest-selling model in the Thonet catalogue, and was brazenly copied by Thonet's competitors.

In 1860 Thonet manufactured its first rocking chair (pictured here). Its design became the Bentwood chair par excellence for many years. It is interesting to note that there was a design precedent: the brass and iron rockers shown at the Crystal Palace London Exhibition in 1851, which were designed and manufactured by R. W. Winfield & Company, Birmingham, England.

The significant factor in Thonet's success and fame was the unique merging of high design standards with the most modern and efficient technology of the time. Bentwood made it possible to produce chairs without complicated carved joints and contours, paving the way for the first mass-produced furniture. In this, Thonet profoundly affected furniture designers, craftspersons, and manufacturers for over one hundred years; his influence continues to be felt today.

The Thonet Brothers business, established in Vienna in the mid-nineteenth century, quickly grew into a vast industry, acquiring forests for materials and employing thousands of workers. Many variations of the Bentwood design have evolved through the years, but the popular Vienna Cafe Chair model is still in production and has been duplicated well over fifty million times.

WILLIAM MORRIS
1834–1899 ENGLAND
SELECTED ACHIEVEMENTS

William Morris became the most prominent and articulate of a group of artists who opposed the debasing effect of industrialization on the human environment. He advocated a return to Gothic craftsmanship, in which people followed their instincts in shaping useful objects, making work a pleasurable activity. Morris claimed that only through this means could human dignity be regained and deep satisfaction achieved. This goal became a lifelong crusade, which came to be called the Arts and Crafts movement. Morris designed furniture, wallpaper, textiles, interiors, and books. In 1890 he founded the Kelmscott Press, an organization dedicated to the production of fine books. He exerted influence as a theorist, crusader, designer, manufacturer, publisher, and client.

Morris is often portrayed as a backward-looking man, out of touch with progress in contemporary manufacturing and mass production. His creative style stands in sharp contrast to the severe functionalism advocated by the Bauhaus. Yet it is of interest that Walter Gropius, head of the famous Bauhaus, wrote in his *New Architecture and the Bauhaus*: ''Ruskin and Morris strove to find a means of reuniting the world of art with the world of work.'' Although the Bauhaus-design products were alien to anything of Morris's own work, they were made in his spirit.

152

Upper: Pimpernel Wallpaper designed by William Morris.
Lower: Plaque ''Favrile'' glass by Louis Comfort Tiffany.

LOUIS COMFORT TIFFANY
1848–1933 UNITED STATES
SELECTED ACHIEVEMENTS

Louis Comfort Tiffany was the son of the founder of the well-known jewelry firm, Tiffany and Company, New York City. Being born and raised in an artistic environment undoubtedly shaped his aesthetic inclinations, which were further refined by his study of art in New York and Paris.

Tiffany's travels and study in Europe made him aware of the Arts and Crafts movement in England and on the continent. Upon his return to New York in 1878, he established the Louis Comfort Tiffany Foundation, an adjunct to his father's Tiffany and Company silversmiths and jewelers. The superb work done by Tiffany's corps of craftspeople reflected his efforts to revive Gothic attitudes toward fine craftsmanship. Tiffany was especially inspired by glassware that featured lustrous iridescent colors. Stained glass, lamps, bowls, and vases were created in the prevailing Art Nouveau style. His famous "favril" vases, bowls, and serving ensembles were spun into elegant flowing forms. Tiffany also designed many interiors for wealthy art patrons, including several rooms in the White House. Tiffany glass may be seen today in the Museum of Modern Art and the Metropolitan Museum in New York.

During Tiffany's illustrious design career, he received international honors from the Societé Nationale des Beaux Arts in France and from the Imperial Fine Arts Society of Japan. His exhibits were extensive: 1900 Paris Exhibition (Gold Award); 1900 Dresden Exhibition (Gold Award); 1901 Turin Exposition (Gold Award); 1904 St. Louis Exposition; 1915 Pan Pacific Exposition, San Francisco (Gold Award); and 1926 Sesqui-Centennial Exposition, Philadelphia (Gold Award).

In 1918, Tiffany established the Louis Comfort Tiffany Fund for art students at Oyster Bay, Long Island, New York, and deeded to it one million dollars and his valuable art collections.

ARTHUR H. MACKMURDO
1851–1942 ENGLAND
SELECTED ACHIEVEMENTS

Arthur Mackmurdo was an English architect, graphic artist, craftsman, and economist. He began his career by studying the crafts, and designing wallpapers, furniture, metalwork, and embroidery. In 1874 he went to Italy with John Ruskin. Remaining there for two years, Mackmurdo gradually shed his Gothic preference in favor of the Renaissance, and made a personal collection of traditional design.

When he returned to England, Mackmurdo set up his own workshops with the help of his pupil, Henry Horne. Later he founded the Century Guild, a loose cooperative association of artists and craftspersons. The aim of the association was to improve English design by returning to craftsmanship with integrity. The style of the Century Guild formed the aesthetic foundation for the Arts and Crafts movement.

Mackmurdo's earliest work exhibits the fact that he was involved with an entirely new design aesthetic, anticipating the Art Nouveau movement by ten years. All the linear characteristics of Art Nouveau may be seen in a chair Mackmurdo designed in 1881, and later on the title page of his book, *Wren's City Churches*, which reveals his innovative and independent spirit.

It may be said that Mackmurdo was the first Modern designer. He made use of natural forms, but always allowed visual values to dominate factual ones.

ALPHONSE MUCHA
1860–1939 CZECHOSLOVAKIA
SELECTED ACHIEVEMENTS

Alphonse Mucha went to Paris in 1887 to complete his education. There he became involved in poster design and emerged one of the leading designers in the Art Nouveau style. His work is filled with flowers on twining stems, bizarre undulations of flowing hair, elaboration of patterns, and the convolutions of creepers and tendrils.

In 1894, Mucha met Sarah Bernhardt and designed the first poster for her. It captivated Bernhardt, and this became the start of a close association with the great actress. Mucha designed the sets and costumes for many of the stage productions in which she appeared.

Mucha's use of color is of particular note. It evokes a soft world of muted shades and delicate tints that often make his long-haired women seem lifeless and ethereal. His work is superbly skillful, beautifully executed, but remote and distant.

Mucha's illustrations are often influenced by great historical predecessors. His mysterious woman who stares dreamily at a smoldering JOB cigarette was influenced by a figure in Michelangelo's ceiling in the Sistine Chapel. A study of Michelangelo's Sybils will reveal the unmistakable influence, right down to the big toe.

After nine years in Paris, Mucha returned to his home in Prague where he resumed the painting of historical subjects.

Upper: Detail; title page for Wren's City Churches by Arthur H. Mackmurdo.
Lower: Detail; menu for La Societe-de-Bienfaisance-Austro-Hongroise by Alphonse Mucha.

HENRY VAN DE VELDE
1863–1957 BELGIUM
SELECTED ACHIEVEMENTS

Henry van de Velde was one of the fathers of the Modern design movement. His work is associated with the innovative and experimental design school called Art Nouveau. He had already established a career in painting when, in 1884, he joined a Brussels organization called Les Vingt, and changed his vocation. There he became a designer of typography, interiors, furniture, and architecture. He expressed his enthusiasm for British ideals and design achievements.

In the Arts and Crafts movement, van de Velde moved ahead with his own ideas. A fine theoretician and philosopher as well as a talented and creative artist, he became one of the leading forces in Art Nouveau design. He favored abstract ornament as opposed to the naturalistic tendencies of Emile Gallé and other French designers. His home, built at Uccle in 1895, presented his personal design ideas and led to commissions in France, Germany, and Holland.

Van de Velde headed the Weimar Art School from 1901 to 1914. This was the school which became the Bauhaus, and, under van de Velde's direction, design education reform was begun. When van de Velde retired, he recommended Walter Gropius to carry on the improvements in design instruction. Gropius credited van de Velde with significantly inspiring Bauhaus theory and style.

Upper: Design for a pendant by Henry Van de Velde.
Lower: Low backed chair by Charles R. Mackintosh.

CHARLES RENNIE MACKINTOSH
1868—1928 SCOTLAND
SELECTED ACHIEVEMENTS

Charles Rennie Mackintosh was a Scottish architect and designer who achieved international recognition for his innovative work in interiors, furniture, lighting fixtures, textile design, display, and graphics.

As a child he traveled to the Continent with his parents and was encouraged to sketch important buildings, which undoubtedly influenced his decision to study architecture.

In 1884 he enrolled in the Glasgow School of Art, studying at night while working days for Scottish architect John Hutchinson. The combination of work/study proved to be an ideal arrangement for Mackintosh, and he received many awards for outstanding work. His association with the art school was warm and productive; he lectured there and from 1894 to 1903 he designed additions to the school. In 1884 he was also honored by the Glasgow Architectural Association with an award of merit. A scholarship award in 1890 allowed him to travel and study in Italy, where he became aware of new design directions in Europe. Several influences may be seen in his work: the intricate linear interlacing of Celtic Art, Art Nouveau, and the philosophy of William Morris who was dedicated to creating closer interrelations of the arts. Mackintosh developed a lasting interest in environmental design, interiors, furniture design, crafts, and graphics. In 1894 he started his own design business in Glasgow, and his first important work was the Cranston Tearoom in Glasgow. The design was comprehensive, including furniture, light fixtures, murals, color, and space. It was during this period that the "FOUR" designers joined forces: Mackintosh, his future wife, her sister, and her sister's fiancé. This partnership dissolved when Mackintosh married in 1900.

Mackintosh's fame was greater abroad than in Scotland. In 1900 and in 1902 he designed furniture and display for international expositions in Vienna and Torino, respectively.

Later three Chicago expositions invited Mackintosh to exhibit: 1923, 1924, and 1925. By 1925 his international reputation as a designer was firmly established, and he became an influence on other artists of the period. Mackintosh's furniture was strongly rectilinear showing an influence of Gothic. Only small touches of curvilinear design were used as accents where supporting elements joined. Of the Glasgow group, Charles Rennie Mackintosh emerged as the most powerful and innovative designer. His work was parallel to, yet divergent from, Art Nouveau.

157

AUBREY BEARDSLEY
1872–1898 ENGLAND
SELECTED ACHIEVEMENTS

Aubrey Beardsley was born and brought up in Brighton, England, a visually stimulating seaside environment, splendidly rich in domestic architecture and design. Certainly Brighton buildings, such as the Dome and the fanciful Royal Pavilion, designed by John Nash, became part of the exotic, imaginative, and bizarre images lodged in Beardsley's mind.

An invalid most of his life, Beardsley had a short but brilliant career as a book illustrator before he died at the age of twenty-six. Long before critics noticed him, Beardsley produced more than five hundred illustrations for a book called *Morte d'Arthur*. Chief among other works Beardsley illustrated were Oscar Wilde's *Salome* (1894), Alexander Pope's *The Rape of the Lock* (1896), and, shortly before his death, Ben Jonson's *Volpone* (1898). Beardsley consistently demonstrated a superb command of compositional mass and scale. His work embodied the spirit of the Art Nouveau style, richly influenced by Japanese prints, embodying an undertone of decadence and morbidity.

Beardsley lived in the Victorian era, an era of gaudiness and hypocrisy, yet he stripped his images to stark black and white. His masterful line drawings accented with contrasting masses of dark demonstrate an arresting visual economy and wit. Beardsley's work survives as a major and still potent influence of Modern art and design.

Salome with Head of St. John by Aubrey Beardsley.

EILEEN GRAY
1878–1976 IRELAND
SELECTED ACHIEVEMENTS

Eileen Gray was an Irish designer who gained fame and recognition for her ability to express the intent of Bauhaus functionalism in a unique way. Her designs of furniture and accessories modified the sober, spare look of the Modern movement, imparting a lighter, elegant touch.

Gray was born in Ireland; her family was part Scotch-Irish nobility with a strong interest in art, which no doubt influenced her education. In 1898 she enrolled in London's Slade School, where she studied drawing. When she went to Paris in 1902, she began a serious study of lacquer, the Oriental craft taught by Sugawara, a Japanese lacquer master. Gray's consequent lacquered screens and tables caught the attention of *Vogue* magazine, which published an article about her in 1917. Her screens designed in this period suggest the influence of Beardsley in their depiction of fantastic mythical figures. Soon, however, Gray began to respond to the architectural style of Gropius and Le Corbusier. It is interesting to note that Gray designed with steel tubing two years before Le Corbusier.

Eileen Gray's work is clean in line, but elegant in spirit, with a freshness and lively inventiveness. At the age of ninety-three she had her first exhibit in London, which was a resounding success. Today many collectors find and purchase her designs. The American painter Frank Stella was so impressed with her London show that he had two of her chair designs reproduced.

Tubular steel furniture designed by Eileen Gray.

LUDWIG MIES VAN DER ROHE
1886—1969 GERMANY, UNITED STATES
SELECTED ACHIEVEMENTS

Mies van der Rohe joined the design studio of Peter Behrens in 1908 where he learned respect for the inherent quality of materials. In 1913 Mies opened his own office and began his long career as an architect of major innovation, leading to elegant steel and glass skyscrapers completely devoid of ornamentation. The use of glass as the exterior skin of a building, a rigid structured system allowing for a ribbon window effect, and the concept of indoor and outdoor flowing space are major contributions by this remarkable designer. This clean uncluttered style that relied upon pure form without superimposed decorative elements later became known as the International Style of architecture. Mies was one of the leading proponents of the style, always guided by his personal motto "less is more."

Mies also became involved in installation design, which led to the design of several famous chairs. The Barcelona chair, a precise chrome and leather design, is still in production and retains a timeless elegance.

Mies was director of the Bauhaus for a short period and left Germany when the pressure of the Nazi regime became too great. He carried on his major architectural work in the United States, both in dramatic skyscrapers such as the Seagram Building in New York, and in individual houses such as the "fifty-by-fifty" house, which has only four support columns, one in the center of each facade.

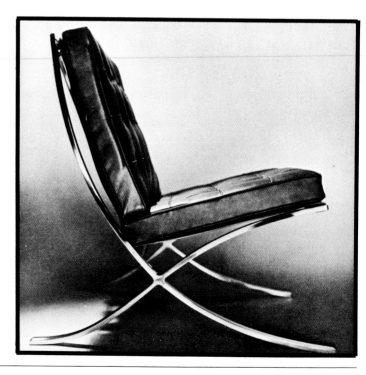

Barcelona Chair. Designer: Ludwig Mies Van der Rohe.

JOSEF ALBERS
1888–1976 GERMANY, UNITED STATES
SELECTED ACHIEVEMENTS

Born in Westphalia, Josef Albers studied at the Royal School of Art in Berlin from 1913 to 1915, and was certified as an art teacher in 1915. He produced lithographs and woodcuts in the German Expressionist manner while teaching at the School of Arts and Crafts in Essen. Later, he studied painting at the Munich Art Academy under Franz Stuch, who had been a teacher of Klee and Kandinsky.

Upon enrolling at the Bauhaus, Albers occupied himself particularly with stained glass painting, developing the technique of sandblasted glass pictures. At the Bauhaus he met his future wife, weaver Anni. In 1925 Albers was appointed master at the Bauhaus, and broadened his designing pursuits to cover typography, glass and metal utility objects, and furniture. He continued teaching at the Bauhaus until it closed in 1933, when he made his first visit to the newly founded Black Mountain College in North Carolina. Albers was one of the first Bauhaus teachers to emigrate to the United States, and was very active in propagating Bauhaus ideas in his new homeland.

When Albers moved on to Yale University in 1950, he became chairman of the Department of Architecture and Design. He began his renowned series of paintings called *Homage to the Square*. His later color experiments are documented in his book, *Interaction of Color*, published in 1963.

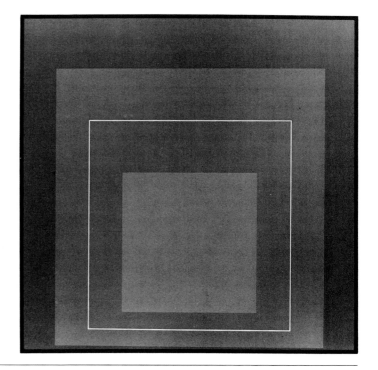

Homage to the Square by Josef Albers.

161

JOHANNES ITTEN
1888–1967 SWITZERLAND
SELECTED ACHIEVEMENTS

Johannes Itten was a Swiss artist and teacher, born in Sudern-Linden in 1888. He studied art with Adolf Hoelzel in Stuttgart from 1913 to 1916, and then opened his own school of art in Vienna. From 1919 to 1923 he taught at the Bauhaus, and introduced the important Preliminary Course, which was obligatory for all students. Itten's basic design course aimed at liberating students from past experiences and prejudices. The course included studio and workshop experiences with materials, as well as instruction in Itten's theory of design contrasts.

The details of Itten's basic course and his theories were later formulated in two publications: *Design and Form, The Basic Course at the Bauhaus* (1964) and *The Art of Color* (1961). Two approaches to color are presented in these works, with more than 155 full-color charts, diagrams, and paintings. First the subjective theory is discussed, dealing with emotional feelings evoked by color. The second approach is objective, exploring intellectual aspects.

The field of color became a major interest for Itten, and he created geometric color abstractions exemplifying his research with color. His original research carried him into the psychology of color perception.

Itten left the Bauhaus in 1923. He founded his own school in Berlin in 1926 and another school for textile designs in Krefeld in 1931.

Forced out of Germany by Nazi pressure, Itten returned to Switzerland, where he directed the Zurich School and Museum of Applied Art from 1938 to 1953.

Itten was honored with two retrospective exhibitions, first at the Stedelijk Museum, Amsterdam, in 1957, and later at the Kunsthaus, Zurich, in 1964.

Light/dark composition in black, white, and grays by Johannes Itten.

162

RAYMOND F. LOEWY
1893—1986 FRANCE, UNITED STATES
SELECTED ACHIEVEMENTS

After beginning his career in advertising layout, illustration, and costume design, Loewy started his own organization of industrial design in 1927, and is considered the father of industrial design. His success was remarkable, and by the late 1930s he had become design consultant to at least one hundred corporations both in the United States and Europe. His firm is now recognized as the largest in the world. Loewy's best-known designs are for trains, automobiles, and airplanes. The streamlined grace and functional economy of his designs appear in such diverse products as electric shavers, toasters, and ball-point pens. On a larger scale, Loewy planned the interior of Lever House in New York City. He wrote several books on industrial design, including: *The Locomotives* (1937), *The Thousand Makers of the 20th Century*, *Industrial Design* (1979), and *Never Leave Well Enough Alone* (1951). Loewy advocated the following practical guidelines for industrial designers: simplify products, make them more economical, easier to maintain and fail-safe so as not to burden further the consumer's already hectic life; avoid unnecessary costly annoyances and irritations; do not indulge in ''yearly model'' changes unless they are justified by sound functional, technological and/or cost advantages.

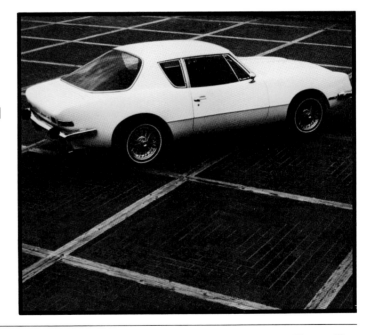

Avanti II. Designer: Raymond Loewy.

163

MARIANNE BRANDT
1893—1983 GERMANY
SELECTED ACHIEVEMENTS

Marianne Brandt was born in Chemnitz, Germany in 1893, and after 1911 she studied art and sculpture at the Grandducal College of Fine Arts in Weimar. While in Norway in 1919 she married, and then went to Paris where she studied for a year. In 1924 Marianne Brandt started her studies at the Bauhaus. After completing the basic courses, she worked in the metal workshop under the direction of Moholy-Nagy. In Weimar and Dessau she developed her famous Kandem lamps as well as metalware, both of which were manufactured commercially. Her designs made revolutionary use of metals and glass, yet for all their unique quality they quickly won public acceptance and established Bauhaus leadership in the area of industrial design. When Moholy-Nagy left the faculty of the Bauhaus, Brandt was invited to succeed him as director of the metal workshop for one year. After this experience she worked temporarily in Walter Gropius's studio in Berlin. From 1929 to 1932 she became a designer for a metal factory in Gotha/Thuringia. Starting in 1949 she taught first at the College of Fine Arts in Dresden and later at the Institute for Applied Art in Berlin, traveling to China with their exhibit in 1953/54. Marianne Brandt's success as an industrial designer realizes the Bauhaus goal of a close working relationship between the designer and industry.

Teapot. Designer: Marianne Brandt.

165

LASZLO MOHOLY-NAGY
1865–1946 HUNGARY
SELECTED ACHIEVEMENTS

Laszlo Moholy-Nagy, a Hungarian-American artist, was born in Hungary in 1895. After qualifying in law at Budapest University, and serving in the army during World War I, he cofounded an Avant-Garde group of painters in Budapest. In 1919 he went to Vienna and came under the influence of Malevich, Lissitsky, and Gabo. In 1921, Moholy-Nagy moved to Berlin, where he began experimenting with collage and photomontage. This experimental interest was in sharp contrast to his previous portraits and landscapes that were permeated with the spirit of cubism.

In Germany, Moholy-Nagy started the experimental work that caught the attention of Walter Gropius, who invited him to teach at the Bauhaus in 1923. There he supervised the metal workshop and taught some of the preparatory courses. Soon his interest turned to photography, and he experimented with photogram, photomontage, and film. He left the Bauhaus in 1928 and settled in Berlin, where he extended his activities to publicity, typography, and designing modern stage sets.

In 1937, after a three-year stay in London, Moholy-Nagy came to Chicago, where he founded the New Bauhaus (later called the Institute of Design), which he directed until his death. His most famous books are *Vision in Motion* (1947) and *The New Vision* (1949).

Moholy-Nagy was one of the most experimental and versatile pioneers in the artistic use of light, movement, photography, and film.

Upper: Visual identity for the Bauhaus Library designed by Laszlo Moholy-Nagy.
Lower: Drawing by Ben Shahn.

BEN SHAHN
1898–1969 LITHUANIA, UNITED STATES
SELECTED ACHIEVEMENTS

Ben Shahn was born in 1898 in Kovno, Lithuania, and emigrated to the United States with his family when he was eight years old. At fifteen he worked as an apprentice in a lithography house, and then went on to study at the Art Students League. Shahn's creative work encompassed a broad range of interests including paintings, drawings, posters, illustrations, murals, books, and photography.

Shahn had a lifelong hatred of injustice, war, and the wrongs of social systems. In actions, words, and images, he expressed his views fearlessly. He gave special attention to the figures in his works, which are characterized by extremely stylized features and outlines, often caricatured. His very personal combination of realism and abstraction creates an apparent naivete.

Shahn was very much drawn to the graphic arts because of their potential for communicating his strong ideas to a large public. Whether it was a series of gouaches on the Sacco and Vanzetti trial, a serigraph about an immigrant family, or subjects out of the Depression years, Shahn's art voiced a strong plea for social conscience.

The Museum of Modern Art in New York City honored Shahn with a retrospective exhibit in 1947. International recognition included prizes at the Sao Paulo Biennial and at the Venice Biennial.

167

ANNI ALBERS
1899—   GERMANY, UNITED STATES
SELECTED ACHIEVEMENTS

Anni Albers is known internationally for her outstanding work in the field of textiles. Her weaving exhibits precision and clarity; her craft skills and design are impeccable. One perceives in her work a mature sensitivity for relationships of shape, texture, line, and form. A remarkable energy and zeal for the process of weaving is evident—from a love of individual threads to the finished woven structure. Her completed textiles are exact, balanced, and harmonized with a remarkable sense of visual order.

Anni Albers was born in Berlin and began her art education in Berlin and Hamburg. In 1922 she entered the Bauhaus, first as a student and later as a professional weaver teaching and doing experimental work with textiles for industry. It was at the Bauhaus where she met, and later married, Josef Albers. From 1933 to 1949 Anni Albers was assistant professor of art at Black Mountain College in North Carolina. Since then she has been lecturing and doing free-lance work at numerous museums and universities. She has been honored by many awards and citations. In 1961 Anni Albers was presented with the gold medal of the American Institute of Architects in the field of craftsmanship. Her book *On Weaving* (1965) is well known and has been a positive influence on a generation of young American weavers.

HERBERT BAYER
1900—1985 AUSTRIA, UNITED STATES
SELECTED ACHIEVEMENTS

After Bayer's formal art study, he apprenticed with an architectural firm where his primary work was in graphic design and typography. From 1921 to 1923 he studied at the Bauhaus at Weimar. In 1924 Bayer began teaching at the Bauhaus as a master instructor in charge of the Bauhaus print shop. After his teaching period, he worked as a painter, photographer, graphic designer, exhibition architect, director of the Dorland Studio, and art director of *Vogue* magazine. From 1938 to 1946 Bayer worked in New York. The period 1946 to 1976 found him involved with the design and architecture for the Aspen Institute for Humanistic Studies in Colorado. Here Bayer's genius for total visual and environmental design was fully challenged. His geometric sculptures and earth-mound designs in open gardens brought an abstract, surrealistic mood to a city environment. He has also designed office buildings and factories, and served as corporate design consultant for the Container Corporation of America from 1946 to 1967. *Double Ascension*, a geometric sculpture, was designed by Bayer for the Arco Plaza in Los Angeles.

Upper: *Woven Silk Tapestry* by Anni Albers. Courtesy the M.I.T. Press.
Lower: A design for an exhibition stand by Herbert Bayer. Courtesy the M.I.T. Press.

169

170

Detail: Poster for Hachard by A. M. Cassandre.

A. M. CASSANDRE
1901–1968 RUSSIA
SELECTED ACHIEVEMENTS

Born in Russia of French parents, A. M. Cassandre was fortunate to have a family able to afford him a college education. Art was his major interest, and from the beginning his work displayed an assertive boldness and impeccable craftsmanship, resulting in a distinct design clarity. Cassandre wrote of his advertising work: "Poster work demands of the painter complete renunciation. If he cannot express himself that way, he has no right to do so." Cassandre perceived his poster work to be clear, powerful, and precise. It is no surprise then that his posters were best-sellers; people could not help but notice his striking visual messages, a decided contrast to the usual jumble of impressions in the everyday environment. Cassandre's design clarity acted as a visual bolt generating an optical shock.

From the 1920s until the approach of World War II, Cassandre's work enlivened walls in France as well as several other countries with visually riveting graphic solutions that engaged the mind as well as the eye. Early in the 1920s, Cassandre established his name in the world of graphic design with his posters *Au Bucheron*, *Pivolo*, and *Dubo, Dubon, Dubonnet*. His imaginative work was so admired that the magazine *Arts et Metiers Graphiques* placed its pages at his disposal. During this period Cassandre designed three typefaces: Bifur (1929), Acier Noir (1935) and Peignot (1937).

In 1926, with two partners, Cassandre founded the advertising agency Alliance Graphique. Cassandre developed an interest in the stage and designed a number of theater productions. Between 1936 and 1938 he made several visits to the United States, working for the Container Corporation of America and *Harper's Bazaar*. In 1936 the Museum of Modern Art had a one-man show of Cassandre's most famous posters and illustrations.

Upon his return to France, Cassandre turned exclusively to painting, but his reputation remains as one of the most influential poster artists of the twentieth century.

MARCEL BREUER
1902—1981 HUNGARY, UNITED STATES
SELECTED ACHIEVEMENTS

Marcel Breuer studied at the Bauhaus as one of its youngest students. At the age of twenty-two he joined the faculty and directed the furniture studies. As a designer, in 1925 he created the first metal tubular chair adapted to mass production. Using the same principle he designed a whole range of furniture. Of all his designs, perhaps the most elegant is the S-shaped cantilever chair still in production today.

In 1928 he left the Bauhaus and moved to Berlin where he worked as a decorator and architect. Dedicated to the functional principles of the Bauhaus, his work in architecture was both bold and practical.

Breuer emigrated first to Britain and then to the United States in 1937. He joined Walter Gropius at Harvard and worked on several projects from 1938 to 1941. In 1946 he opened his own design studio in New York and has completed many major architectural commissions including: the UNESCO building in Paris (1958), the Church of St. John's Abbey, Minnesota (1961), IBM Research Center at La Gaude, France (1962), and Whitney Museum of American Art in New York (1966).

APPLICATION OF THE HUMAN FIGURE TO A CONTROL CONSOLE FOR THE BELL TELEPHONE LABORATORIES, INC.

172

Upper: Wassily Chair. Designer: Marcel Breuer.
Lower: Design study, Application of the Human Figure to a Control Console for the Bell Telephone Laboratories, Inc., by Henry Dreyfus.

Dreyfus has been one of the major forces in the field of industrial design in the United States since 1930. He was successful in convincing big industry that good design earns larger profits. The opening of his first industrial design office in New York in 1929, just prior to the Depression years, turned out to be a remarkable advantage. Industry, for the first time, sought out designers who could help sell products by making objects more attractive and efficient. In 1933 Dreyfus designed a refrigerator for General Electric whose motor was in the bottom instead of sitting on top. His work for the Crane Company set a trend toward built-in plumbing fixtures. He has designed Hoover vacuum cleaners, Eversharp pens, Royal typewriters, and graphic design layouts for *Time, Reader's Digest,* and *McCall.*

Of special note is his invention of the "Humanscale," a series of charts detailing human movements. Included are such figures as the proper dimension for all types of seating, the most efficient height for a doorknob or a towel dispenser, and the depth needed for toe space under a counter. This information is helpful to engineers, architects, industrial designers, interior designers and furniture designers.

Dreyfus kept his office small, stressing teamwork and research. To every problem, he applied a five-point yardstick; utility and safety, maintenance, cost, sales appeal, and appearance.

GYORGY KEPES
1906– HUNGARY
SELECTED ACHIEVEMENTS

Gyorgy Kepes, a Hungarian-American artist, was born in Selyp, Hungary, and studied art at the Budapest Academy of Fine Arts. In the early 1930s he worked in Berlin and London on film, stage, and exhibition design. In 1937, Kepes came to the United States to head the light and color department at the Institute of Design in Chicago. Kepes also taught at North Texas State Teachers College and at the Massachusetts Institute of Technology. His first one-man show was in 1939 at the Katherine Kuh Gallery in Chicago. Among other commissions, Kepes created murals for the Harvard University Graduate Center and the Royal Dutch Airlines offices in New York City.

A prolific writer, Kepes' ideas have been set forth in several major books: *Language of Vision* (1944), *The New Landscape in Art and Science* (1967), and *Education of Vision* (1965). He states clearly that "the primary and necessary aim of education is the carefully sequential interplay between sensory, imaginative awareness, and disciplined, scientific knowledge."

174

Upper: Detail; *Rhythmic Light Mural* by Georgy Kepes. Courtesy the M.I.T. Press.
Lower: Woven casement cloth. Designer: Alexander Girard.

ALEXANDER GIRARD
1907—   UNITED STATES
SELECTED ACHIEVEMENTS

Alexander Girard is by profession an architect, but architecture has not been his major preoccupation. For over fifty years he has been designing exhibitions of modern furniture, indigenous folk arts, and textiles as well as interiors, showrooms, and restaurants. In all his work, color and pattern are used in joyous profusion. He is above all a great colorist.

After graduating from the Architectural Association in 1929, his first projects showed a tendency to combine Bauhaus austerity with touches of handcraft. By 1935 Girard was seen as a young star in modern interior design. He was quoted as saying, "My primary objective is to give the public not a 'modern' convulsed by mechanistic obsessions or standardized into a sterile formality, but a reasonable and sane functionalism, tempered by what my critics call 'irrational frivolity,' which I prefer to call aesthetic functionalism."

While working for Detrola Corporation he came in contact with Charles Eames, and a long friendship began. Through Eames, Girard met George Nelson, then design director for Herman Miller Co., and Nelson brought Girard into the company. Girard's work with fabrics was influenced by the extensive traveling he began to do in the 1950s. He has developed a collection of over 100,000 artifacts from countries all over the world that also influence his design work. The strong flavor of Latin America permeated his design of La Fonda del Sol restaurant in New York. Its design was revolutionary, grand, and total: floors, walls, lighting, color, menus, tile—everything was selected and designed by Girard down to the buttons on the waiters' jackets. Girard's spirited and colorful work has enlivened design and reawakened the human capacity for sensuous enjoyment.

175

176

Plywood and metal base dining chair designed by the office of Charles and Ray Eames.

CHARLES AND RAY EAMES
1907–1978, 1912–1988 UNITED STATES
SELECTED ACHIEVEMENTS

Charles and Ray Eames, husband-and-wife partners since 1941, were designers, film-makers, photographers, and architects. True innovators, they combined aesthetics with new technology to develop completely new concepts in seating. The Eames molded ply-wood chair has received widespread acclaim not only for its innovative use of material, but for its purity of form and physical comfort. Ever attuned to new processes and materials, the Eameses introduced in 1949 a molded fiberglass shell chair that set a new standard in lightweight chair design. The Eames furni-ture collection, produced exclusively by Her-man Miller, increased over the years to in-clude wire mesh chairs, the signature lounge chair and ottoman, airport seating, an execu-tive chaise, and a soft pad aluminum group.

In addition to furniture design, the Eameses developed an interest in exhibition design. Charles Eames and Eero Saarinen entered the 1940 exhibit and competition "Organic Design and Home Furnishings" at the Museum of Modern Art in New York. Later, in 1946, the Museum of Modern Art presented "New Furniture by Charles Eames." The show was very successful and served to advance public awareness of the Eames furniture, as well as the Eameses' talent for mounting a stunning show. Among the earliest Eames exhibition designs was a multi-screen slide presentation for the 1959 American National Exhibition in Moscow. Their grid-like series of simultaneous slides, depicting aspects of the everyday lives of Americans, was well-received by Soviet viewers. This international success led to exhibitions and visual presen-tations for IBM, such as "Mathematica," dis-played at the California Museum of Science and Industry in 1961, and "A Computer Per-spective," shown at the IBM Exhibition Cen-ter, New York, in 1971.

The short films made by the Eameses range from complex mathematical presentations such as "Powers of Ten," to a whimsical film based on the Eames' collection of toys, "Toccata for Toy Trains" (1957), with original music by Elmer Bernstein. The famous Eames home in Santa Monica, California, was pre-sented visually in a short film called "House" (1955). Of special interest to design students are the films "Textiles and Ornaments of In-dia" (1955), and "Day of the Dead" (1957). In 1964 the Eameses produced a multi-media show called "Think" for the New York World's Fair, using twenty-two screens with carefully sequenced slides and motion pic-ture films. The impact was dazzling, and reached a high in complex exhibition design. People lined up for hours to see this remark-able show.

Finally, their love of toys led the Eameses to experiment with and design delightful con-structions such as the "House of Cards" and the "Do-Nothing Machine," which runs on solar energy.

177

GEORGE NELSON
1908—1986 UNITED STATES
SELECTED ACHIEVEMENTS

George Nelson was originally educated as an architect. He won a Prix de Rome award along with his diploma, which enabled him to study and travel for two years in Europe. In addition to the treasures of the past, he discovered the modern movement in architecture and interviewed as many pioneers of the movement as possible. His interviews with Corbusier and Mies van der Rohe were published when Nelson returned to the United States. On the strength of these perceptive reports, he was offered a position on *Architectural Forum*. Nelson eventually became co-managing editor, and during this period he wrote for *Time, Fortune,* and *Life* magazines.

In 1947 Nelson opened his own office of architecture and design in New York. During this period, Nelson accepted an offer as designer for Herman Miller, an interior design firm, and began with intensity to design and assemble the first Herman Miller collection. Nelson developed and refined the Herman Miller image through designing the early showrooms, full-page advertisements, and the symbol *M*, their logo. He was responsible for recruiting Eames and Girard; from then on they stimulated and cross-fertilized each other's work. Nelson, however, put the show on the road. It is as a designer of exhibitions and films that Nelson is most dazzling. In 1952 the three designers created an impressive and daring three-screen slide and film production that stimulated and instructed viewers with a prodigious array of images. Nelson has continued to be a prolific designer of furniture, desks, chairs, sofas, tables, storage units, and a classic chaise longue design. Simultaneously, he has taught at Harvard University and Pratt Art Institute.

HANS WEGNER
1914— DENMARK
SELECTED ACHIEVEMENTS

It has been said that more than any other furniture designer of our time, Hans Wegner stands for economy, refinement of design, and perfection in execution. His career started at the age of seventeen when he apprenticed in a small furniture workshop where he learned to make everything from coffins to writing desks. Later he studied with Johannes Hansen, a renowned Danish furniture designer who admired Wegner's work so much that he gave him a free hand in design.

His early chairs were rather stiff and straight, but as he developed his work became graceful and sculptural. Two of his later chairs have become modern classics: the "wishbone chair" and the "cowhorn chair." In the 1940s Wegner's simple, modest, modern designs were honored by Danish museums. In 1947 Wegner's work became known abroad, and in 1965 Georg Jensen in New York City exhibited a retrospective showing of Wegner's most famous designs. An article by Jere Osgood in the July, 1965, issue of *Crafts Horizon* magazine stated:

> Wegner's chairs fulfill beautifully the requirements of function and structure. No point is missed in the detailing and the pieces generate a feeling of warmth of a natural material. The designs stand apart in a room, yet serve as superb adjuncts to the ever increasing examples of our machine technology.

Upper: Trademark, Herman Miller, Inc. Designer: George Nelson.
Lower: Chair by architect Hans J. Wegner and cabinetmaker Johannes Hansen.

PAUL RAND
1914—   UNITED STATES
SELECTED ACHIEVEMENTS

Paul Rand is among America's most distinguished graphic designers, having received acclaim in the United States and abroad. The major body of his work was produced during the 1940s and 1950s when he was most influential. His style is characterized by a teetering, asymmetrical balance, and he relies on abstract or abstracted imagery. Symbolism also appears frequently in his work, balanced by a subtle humor that imbues his art with a distinct light-heartedness.

Among Rand's numerous honors and achievements are the gold medal of the American Institute of Graphic Arts and an award from the New York Art Directors Club. He has taught at Yale University, Pratt Art Institute, the School of the Boston Museum of Art, and the Philadelphia College of Art, and is an adviser in art education for New York University. Rand has been art director for *Esquire, Coronet,* and *Apparel Arts* magazines, during which time he established his reputation as an innovative problem solver. Leading organizations have availed themselves of his graphic design abilities: Olivetti, ABC, United Parcel, the Museum of Modern Art, and the U.S. Department of the Interior. Mr. Rand serves as a consultant for IBM, Westinghouse, and other corporations. His book *Some Thoughts on Design* (1970) expresses his philosophy of art in a clear, direct manner.

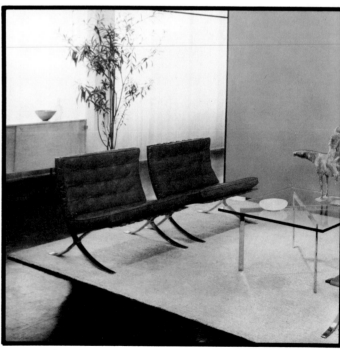

Upper: Trademark, T.V. Billboard, Westinghouse. Designer: Paul Rand.
Lower: Detail; the New York showroom of Knoll Associates Inc., 1951, designed by Florence Schust Knoll Bassett.

FLORENCE SCHUST KNOLL BASSETT
1917—   UNITED STATES
SELECTED ACHIEVEMENTS

Florence Bassett has earned a reputation for being one of the most influential contemporary designers of furniture and interiors. Her work demonstrates the finest use of space, an impeccable sense of clean, uncluttered detail, perceptive scale, and a mixture of pure form enriched by judicious use of alluring texture. Through Knoll Associates in New York, she helped to popularize the International Style by establishing Knoll showrooms in major cities in the United States. Her style and visual judgment set the pace for contemporary and sophisticated interior design all over America.

Florence Bassett was born in Michigan. She studied with Eliel Saarinen at Kingswood School and later at Cranbrook Academy of Art in Michigan. Advanced art study was with Mies van der Rohe at the Illinois Institute of Technology graduating in 1941. Her first professional experience was with architectural firms in Boston and New York. While in New York she joined Knoll Associates; in 1946 she married Hans Knoll. Upon his death in 1955 she carried on as president of the firm. Bassett was responsible for the interiors of banks, university dormitories, showrooms, and office buildings. She resigned from Knoll in 1965. Today she continues her design work from studios in Florida and Vermont.

ETTORE SOTTSASS
1917–   AUSTRIA
SELECTED ACHIEVEMENTS

Ettore Sottsass was born in Austria in 1917, where he was trained as an architect, but he gained recognition as a first-rate designer for Olivetti, the Italian corporation famous for its clean, fastidious, functional products. Along with his well-paid design work for Olivetti, Sottsass experimented with, and developed his own personal flair for design, which eventually flowered into a highly imaginative and playful style called Memphis.

The Memphis movement began as an experiment in museum exhibition design, aiming to present fast images typical of the electronics world. From the beginning one can detect an interest in the fleeting and impermanent aspects of the world today. Sottsass has expressed his fascination with brief images in design, and, compatible with that concept, he has predicted that Memphis will be short-lived. He said, "I would be terrified that Memphis may carry on for ten years, or even for five."

In the late 1970s Sottsass established a design firm in Milan, which he named "Il Nuovo Design"; the firm was also called "Studio Alchymia." A team of designers banded together to offer design alternatives. The designs coming out of this team enterprise were eccentric, arbitrary, and of dubious function: the antithesis of modern design.

Upper: Eastside lounge chair designed by Ettore Sottsass.
Lower: Sudler, Hennessey & Lubalin logo. Designer: Herb Lubalin. Finished lettering by John Pistilli.

HERB LUBALIN
1918–1981 UNITED STATES
SELECTED ACHIEVEMENTS

Herb Lubalin was born in New York City in 1918. He graduated from Cooper Union in 1931, and designed displays for the New York World's Fair the same year. For several years he designed for *Men's Wear* magazine and, in 1964, he set up a design firm bearing his name.

Lubalin was a generalist whose graphic design activity spanned the entire range of graphic communication: advertising, editorial design, trade marks, packaging, posters, book jacket design, and typeface design. His major typeface designs include Avant Garde, Lubalin Graphic, and Serif Gothic. Abandoning the normal rules of typography in the 1950s, he began to overlap letters, blow them up to large size, and squeeze the space between words. Legibility was often sacrificed for visual impact.

Lubalin used "graphic expressionism," his euphemism for the use of typography, not just as a means of setting words on a page, but as a way of expressing an idea in order to elicit an emotional response from the viewer.

As a recipient of more than 500 awards of excellence from professional organizations, and as a member of the New York Art Directors Club Hall of Fame, Lubalin's genius as a typographic designer is clearly recognized.

SAUL BASS
1920—   UNITED STATES
SELECTED ACHIEVEMENTS

After serving as art director for several advertising agencies in New York City, Saul Bass went to California and established his own firm in 1952. Designing for such large corporations as Alcoa, Celanese, Rockwell International, AT&T, Fuller Paints, and United Airlines has made him famous for his work in establishing corporate visual identity.

Bass also became involved in designing titles and title sequences for films and has developed an innovative film design form. Some of his major film titles and opening sequences appear in *Man with the Golden Arm, Around the World in Eighty Days, The Big Country, Vertigo, Anatomy of a Murder, Exodus,* and *West Side Story.* In 1964 he directed two short films for the New York World's Fair, *The Searching Eye* (Kodak) and *From Here to There* (United Airlines). Then in 1968 he directed *Why Man Creates*, a twenty-five minute film exploring creative vision in an amusing yet penetrating way. Recently he directed a full-length feature film, *Phase IV,* for Paramount Pictures. Examples of Bass's work are in the permanent collections of the Museum of Modern Art, the Library of Congress, the Smithsonian Institute, the Prague Museum, the Stedelijk Museum (Amsterdam), and others throughout the world.

Catalog design for Pyramid Films by Saul Bass.

JACK LENOR LARSEN
1927– UNITED STATES
SELECTED ACHIEVEMENTS

Jack Lenor Larsen is recognized internationally as a leader in the world of fabric design, an innovator in the field of environmental design, and a developer of new textile treatments. He created the first successful diagonally woven fabric, and revised the ancient technique of shaped weaving. Larsen converted costly hand-weaving procedures to the power loom, enabling him to expand the design potential of mass-production weaving.

Larsen was born in Seattle in 1927. He attended the University of Washington, and received his B.F.A. in 1950. In 1951, he earned his M.F.A. at the Cranbrook Academy of Art. He went from there to New York City, and established his own Jack Lenor Larsen Design Studio in 1958. His first major commission was the design of the draperies in Park Avenue Lever House by Skidmore-Owings and Merrill, which has become a landmark of the Modern movement in the United States. Larsen's success as a fabric designer soon allowed him to branch out with franchises in Zurich, Stuttgart, and Paris. Today Larsen is a dominant force in international fabric and textile design.

Larsen's work is in the Museum of Modern Art, the Metropolitan Museum, and the Victoria and Albert Museum in London. He has coauthored the following books: *Elements of Weaving* (1967), *Beyond Craft, The Art Fabric* (1973), *Fabrics for Interiors* (1975), and *The Dyer's Art* (1977).

Interplay, a Rovana knit casement fabric. Designer: Jack Lenor Larsen.

185

SEYMOUR CHWAST
1931–   UNITED STATES
SELECTED ACHIEVEMENTS

At the age of four, Seymour Chwast amazed his family and friends by drawing cartoons and complete comic books. Much later he studied illustration and design at Cooper Union, where his classmates included Milton Glaser and Edward Sorel. After graduation, Chwast, Glaser, and Sorel founded Push Pin Studios. The Push Pin attitude was, to a large measure, shaped by the Chwast influence; it is sometimes difficult to disentangle his style from that of the studio.

Chwast is a master of both clean contour line and textured free-flowing line. His flat, bold color is controlled to create a sophisticated comic book quality. Chwast often deals in satiric subtleties, combined with a sense of wit and social conscience, sometimes sentimental and broadly humanistic.

Chwast's work displays evidence of his keen interest in many historical styles, drawing material and inspiration from all periods, absorbing historical precedents and reshaping visual stimuli in his unique graphic expression. Chwast has written: "While I am not particularly disposed to any style or type of image, I still follow the basic elements of design in my work."

186

Upper: The letter "A" from an alphabet designed by Seymour Chwast.
Lower: The letter "A" from an alphabet designed by Milton Glaser.

MILTON GLASER
1929–   UNITED STATES
SELECTED ACHIEVEMENTS

Milton Glaser is an American graphic designer, born in New York City and educated at the High School of Music and Art in New York. In 1951 Glaser graduated from Cooper Union, then continued his art study at the Academy of Fine Arts in Bologna, Italy.

After studying art in Europe on a Fulbright Scholarship, Glaser produced a series of lithographs. In 1954, he, Seymour Chwast, and Edward Sorel formed Push Pin Studios, which gained an excellent reputation in the field of graphic design. Glaser produces illustrations, designs for advertising, book jackets, and books. He also teaches at the School of Visual Arts in New York City.

When Glaser entered the graphic design field, there was a rigid distinction between the functions of the designer and the illustrator. Glaser refused to accept this separation. His own work, integrating design and illustration, is often a mixture of bold visual fun and forceful urgency. Glaser's commissions range from IBM, Olivetti, Time-Life, and Graphis, to RCA and CBS. He has received international recognition, and was the winner of the Gold Medal of the American Institute of Graphic Arts in 1972. His work is in the permanent design collection of the Museum of Modern Art in New York City.

187

IKKO TANAKA
1930–   JAPAN
SELECTED ACHIEVEMENTS

Ikko Tanaka studied design at Kyoto Municipal College of Art, and began his design career in 1950 when he joined Kanegafuchi Mills as a textile designer. From 1952 to 1958 he worked as a graphic designer, and in 1960 he became art director of the Nippon Design Center in Tokyo. In 1963 he established his own design studio in Tokyo, and that same year the Museum of Modern Art in New York City selected four of Tanaka's posters for its permanent collection.

Tanaka has received international recognition with invitational exhibitions in the Netherlands and in Poland. In 1964 he designed the symbol and the medals for the Tokyo Olympics. The Government Pavilion at the Osaka International Fair Exposition in 1970 was also his design. His work reflects the Japanese spirit of refinement and great beauty, yet it is fully contemporary in its use of color, line, and proportion. One sees these qualities in all of Tanaka's work—books, trademarks, folders, posters, packages, and display.

Tanaka is one of the most outstanding, yet representative, graphic designers of Japan. Not only is he famous in Japan; he gained world-wide recognition for his excellence in portraying the Noh Drama in poster form. Tanaka's graphic talents communicate the beauty of things Japanese to the world at large.

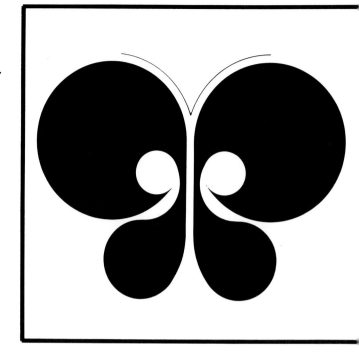

Trademark, Hanae Mori Knit. Designer: Ikko Tanaka.

Part V

Design Projects

The authors believe that there are essential and valuable studio experiences capable of sharpening visual perception and stimulating visual imagination. Carefully planned basic design projects establish a design sense that will long serve the designer as visual alertness is practiced and refined. Each of the arts demands fundamental awareness, attitudes and skills gained through vigorous and carefully planned exercise. In the case of dance, the beginning student is required to master a series of basic movements which become instilled in the muscles and nervous system. The body then instinctively moves with an acquired grace and reliable dance integrity. A discipline of movement is established, then kept alive by the professional dancer through continuing work. Acquired control and finesse will be revealed in any dance form the dancer undertakes, and the discipline of movement established early becomes clearly evident to the observer. Such discipline serves as a freeing agent enabling the dancer to undertake a variety of dance challenges.

The work undertaken in basic design helps to establish a vigorous visual discipline comparable to the physical discipline of the dancer. Basic design must be truly fundamental, a preparation enabling the student to move with confidence into a specific chosen design field. In the study of design it is important that new and demanding patterns of thought and perception be awakened, encouraged, and exercised, so that visual values emerge as having primary structural purpose, not merely superficial or decorative. To accomplish this goal, the student must seek and recognize the value of PRIMARY, FIRST-HAND, DIRECT VISUAL EXPERIENCE. A shift is necessary because all words are SECONDARY experience, once removed from actual SEEING, TOUCHING, HEARING, SMELLING, and TASTING things encountered in the environment. Learning to value and to open up to primary experience is to increase intake and to sharpen perception. Educating the senses becomes the first priority.

The visual arts and DESIGN are based firmly on firsthand experiences, and can be expressed only in ways that are intrinsically visual. Attention is focused on relationships between colors, values, lines, textures, between solid masses arranged in space. These are ideas understood not in literary form, but visual ideas understood through the senses. Too long it has been assumed that everything thought and felt can be expressed in words; that verbal facility leads to precise and constructive thinking. Verbal discipline and finesse in word usage is revered as a badge of academic success and achievement. Such esteem for only the literary form of education holds hazards and may be a serious

drawback. Too much reliance on secondhand experience can create harmful dislocation and alienation, causing one to lose touch with and blunt the ability to savor firsthand experiences in the environment.

The basic structure of design has been explored by many nineteenth and twentieth century designers; although there are perceptible variations in content and approach, there is ample ground for agreement. The beginnings of a critical examination of design education emerged in the mid-nineteenth century during the Victorian period. Henry Cole, a leader in English design reform, saw the necessity for revitalizing the curriculum of the Royal Academy of Art. The Royal Academy dominated British art with powerful academic emphasis on the study of historical design forms as the main staple. Cole's was a timid effort resulting in a slightly revised design curriculum. His efforts failed to recognize the essential and underlying principles of design, and continued to rely on drawing skill (largely from plaster casts of classic sculptures) and historical motifs which did little to kindle true inventiveness and imagination.

Early in the twentieth century, two innovative men in the United States cooperated in developing

an alternative to "Academic" art study. Ernest Fenellosa, Curator of Oriental Art at the Boston Museum, and Arthur W. Dow, Columbia University, began to analyze Oriental art, particularly Japanese works. The basic design elements and principles that these men identified, formed the basis for a new approach to the study of art. Drawing was not to be ignored or seen as an end in itself, but rather it was viewed as a means of creative expression. Design problems became the dominant concern of the new curriculum created to develop visual judgment, selectivity, and ultimately "creative power." This new instructional method marked an innovative turning away from slavish academic copying toward the freeing of creative energy.

In 1918 Johannes Itten joined the faculty of the Bauhaus in Weimar, Germany, where he developed the basic course described and illustrated in his book, *Design and Form*. Itten included the use of both drawing and design combined to exercise visual awareness and creative invention.

From the first innovative basic design course by Johannes Itten to current developments, the principal emphasis has been to encourage VISUAL THINKING. The development of visual thinking depends upon three essential components which are vital to design study:

1. understanding the visual elements and principles;
2. exercising imaginative problem-solving, and;
3. developing technical skills.

A successful study of design will rely on a balanced combination of these three essentials. Some assignments may concentrate on mastery of color mixing and color interaction; other projects may focus attention on LINE, VALUE, TEXTURE; others may emphasize proportion and spacing awareness—purely formal decision-making. Other assignments may challenge imaginative powers, calling into play freewheeling inventiveness. A possible danger occurs when the freewheeling inventive assignments become so alluring that formal disciplined work is minimized. On the other extreme, emphasis on purely formal problem-solving may dominate, to the detriment of the more playful aspects. So, a balanced mix will surely be the most productive. The merging of FORM, IMAGINATION and TECHNIQUE is essential. To organize an idea takes a very particular kind of imaginative vision. There are those in art who associate imaginative inventiveness with one sort of expression—the spontaneous free-for-all. Sadly, the result may remain nothing more than a frivolous action lacking visual clarity and cohesiveness. The student should cherish spontaneity but learn to continue with an idea to a well designed conclusion. The merging of design form and imagination is the guiding idea behind the development of BASIC DESIGN study leading to a disciplined way of working.

The following series of assignments has been developed by the authors, combining shared teaching experience. The resulting studio projects also represent a careful blending of the three essential visual components and are grouped under separate design categories.

With the exception of the visual research assignments where figurative subjects are called for, the predominant study themes are nonfigurative. Working with lean, spare visual elements helps the beginning design student to concentrate on purely formal design considerations. Full attention is directed to essential visual relationships of line, value, color, spacing, grouping, and movement. As visual discipline develops, the eye becomes sharply perceptive. A critical keenness is realized, an ability that will grow and deepen as the designer continues to mature.

VISUAL AWARENESS
Collection: The Basic Elements—192

VISUAL RESEARCH AND IMAGINATION
Abstract Images—194
Bridge Abstraction—196
Wire Animal—198
Articulated Plant Form—200
Textured Line Imprint—202

VISUAL VOCABULARY—LINE
Brush Calligraphy—204
Line and Shape Structure—206
Line Contrast—208
Balsa Linear Cube—210
Three-dimensional Line and Shape—212

VISUAL VOCABULARY—VALUE
Black and Gray Squares—214
Line and Value Structure—216
Cube Structure in Black and Grays—218

VISUAL VOCABULARY—COLOR
Value and Intensity Charts—220
Colorful Squares—222
Collage Paint Match—224

VISUAL VOCABULARY—SHAPE AND FORM
Outline and Solid Shapes—226
Angular Shape Structure—228
Metamorphosis—230
Contrast Collage—232
Radial Bas-relief—234
Cube Surface Design—236
Monolithic Form—238

VISUAL VOCABULARY—TEXTURE AND PATTERN
Texture Samples—240
Texture Composition—242
Rhythmic Pattern—244
Word Pattern—246

VISUAL VOCABULARY—SPACE
Positive to Negative Transformation—248
Space Collage—250

INTERACTION AND ORDER
Proportion: Exercises in Visual Relationships—252
Emphasis—254
Movement—256
Balance—258
Repetition—260

RESPONSE AND EXPRESSION
Leaf Collage—262
Letter Form Collage—264
Four Seasons Sun Symbol—266
Mood Collage—268

Collection:
The Basic Elements

Task:

Search in current and/or old magazines for photographs or drawings which are predominantly 1) line; 2) value; 3) color; 4) texture; and 5) pattern.

1. Selection may be an entire photograph; more likely it will be a particular part of a large photograph, so cropping will be important.

2. Select at least 25–30 examples of each of the five elements above. Put them aside in a folder or envelope.

3. Before final assembly and presentation, edit the collection severely, selecting only the highest quality examples for display, discarding borderline items. Display and arrange 12–15 of the best choices or finds on separate boards—one visual element represented on each 15″ × 20″ board.

4. Plan a well-designed layout of your choices:
   a. An asymmetrical, balanced arrangement will provide the most flexibility.
   b. The final grouping will no doubt result in a variety of sizes. To avoid random clutter, align and coordinate edges in order to create line edge continuity.

5. Shift and group until a well-designed presentation is achieved.

6. Adhere examples to board, including lettering if desired.

7. This assignment is a semester or term assignment to be submitted at the end; it may be considered a final, visual examination.

Materials:

Magazine photographs
Scissors, exacto-knife
   Warning: Use extreme caution when working with sharp instruments.
Straightedge
Glue, or dry-mount paper
Five 10″ × 15″ mat boards

Outcomes:

—Learn to use pure vision to perceive visual elements, a discipline that begins to liberate the need for object-mindedness, seeing visual qualities entirely free from subject matter considerations.
—Develop an appreciation and understanding of the basic design elements.

Text References:

Expanding the perceptive eye, Chapter 1
Visual research, Chapter 2

A collection and layout of line examples.

Abstract Images

Task:

Develop a composition of abstracted images based on telephone and power poles, wires, insulators, and conductors.

1. Begin this project by making at least five accurate information drawings of telephone and power pole components based on careful direct observation.

2. Develop a series of ideas using thumbnail trials that are basically linear in composition but include detailed interpretations which are based on the observed images of the power pole environment (connectors, insulators, etc.).

3. By careful selection, simplification, and alteration, create imaginative imagery, yet retain the essence and look of the particular industrial products.

4. Refine and perfect the proportions, intersections, and positive-to-negative interactions to achieve a unique design.

5. Make a final 10″ × 12″ line drawing on tracing paper. On illustration board, paint an appropriate background. Transfer the line design to the painted background and render the design in contrasting hues to the background.

Materials:

Sketch paper and tracing paper
Illustration board
Opaque water-based paint
Brushes
Pencil and ruling pen
Straightedge

Outcomes:

—Increase ability to observe, record, and interpret.
—Provide experience in translating informational drawings into imaginative design which requires a balance in retaining essential characteristics of observed images, and at the same time exercising imaginative freedom.

Text References:

Environmental images, p. 18
Abstraction, pp. 22, 128
Discussion and examples of abstraction, pp. 28–29
Abstraction as surface enrichment (upper), p. 95
Abstraction stylization, pp. 129, 170

An informational drawing: simplification and alteration.

Bridge Abstraction

Task:

Develop and render in color an abstract design related to research on bridge structures.

1. Collect photos and/or accurate drawings of bridges—whole spans or parts.

2. Make several thumbnail sketches of distinctive bridge characteristics in pencil.

3. Refine and develop the best idea in pencil line and value.

4. Enlarge on sturdy tracing paper, refining and adding important detail. Allow the idea to move toward abstraction and away from imitation, yet retaining essential bridge structural elements.

5. Trace the line design onto 8″ × 12″ illustration board.

6. Render in two basic hues with as many values as needed. Final rendering should exhibit technical control and appropriate finish.

Outcomes:

—Practice in visual research.
—Experience the demanding work of extracting essential structural characteristics, the basis for cohesive design form.
—Understand the importance of the visual elements in translating research into finished design.

Text References:

Visual research, Chapter 2
Creating a new image, Chapter 3, p. 22
From actual to designed image, p. 6
Stages of abstraction, p. 29
Imaginative designed images, pp. 57 (upper right) & (lower right), 63
Fragmented figures, p. 70
Designed symbols, p. 106

Materials:

Newsprint paper, illustration board, tracing paper
Opaque water-based paint
Soft pencil and brushes
Plastic palette

An inventive abstraction based on bridge information.

Visual Research and Imagination

Wire Animal

Task:

Construct a linear abstract animal based on the structure of a real animal.

1. Research is the key to the success of this project. Look for books on animals and on the bone structure of animals.

2. Begin by making pencil sketches using lines to describe the volume and structure of the animal selected. The degree of abstraction may vary. Select those essential elements to create a unique animal form.

3. Once the sketch is refined, select the wire or wires to be used to turn the linear sketch into linear form. The size should not exceed 500 cubic inches. Be sure the wires are compatible and can be soldered together using a simple soldering iron. Go beyond the simple outline to create form. Since there is no skin to cover the form, the transparency of wires in space defining and describing form becomes an intriguing task.

4. View the animal from all sides. Watch the line quality of the wire. Do not accept unwanted kinks or bumps in the wire. Carefully control bends to build continuity of line, and be aware of connecting transitions from part to part. Be sure the animal will stand securely on a flat surface.

Materials:

Wire
Solder and flux and soldering iron
Warning: Use extreme caution when working with the hot soldering iron. Use solder and flux that is free of cadmium, lead and fluoride.
Wire-cutter and needle-nose pliers
Paper and pencil

Outcomes:

—Learn to build three-dimensional transparent form, using line as the basic element.
—Increase awareness of how abstraction can be used to create unique form.
—Learn to transfer a two-dimensional sketch into a three-dimensional form.

Text References:

Visual research, p. 15
Abstraction, pp. 28, 63, 80, 127
Shape and form, p. 58

Abstract animal forms built on careful observations.

Articulated Plant Form

Task:

Using a number of flat shapes (planes) construct a three-dimensional plant form that is based on both the external, and internal structure.

1. Begin visual research at a market or vegetable stand. Focus on fruits, vegetables, nuts, gourds or seed pods that are primarily monolithic in structure. A final selection, however, will be determined by cutting open the object to discover the internal substance. The inside structure should allow for an interplay of design detail with overall form building. A quick observation of the inside of a potato will reveal little of interest as contrasted to the inside of a pomegranate.

2. Cut the selected object, if possible, into a number of slices or planes. Using colored pencils develop a series of sketches by drawing a series of planes to describe both volume and structure.

3. By using both simplification and alteration, push or pull the ideas as far from the natural state of the real object as you wish without losing its identity.

4. When the sketch idea is finished and many of the design decisions have been made, the process of constructing the three-dimensional objects begins.

5. Cut the flat shapes (planes) out of illustration board and use Bristol board or paper for the curved planes.

6. With pins or masking tape try an assemblage of the parts to make up the three-dimensional whole. Sand edges if necessary.

7. Disassemble and paint the individual parts with water-based paint emphasizing details, texture and color derived from close inspection of the real object.

8. Reassemble the parts and glue and pin together until the glue sets.

9. Retouch painted areas and add detail to finish the articulated plant form.

Materials:

Sketch paper
Illustration board
Four-ply Bristol board and textured papers
Masking tape and glue
Opaque water-based paint and brushes
Exacto-knife and scissors
  Warning: Use extreme caution when working with sharp instruments.
Sandpaper

Outcomes:

—Increase awareness of natural forms as a source of design inspiration.
—Learn to interpret and abstract from a real object.
—Increase ability to use design elements to create unique expressive form.
—Explore the potential of the additive process of form building.

Text References:

Environmental images, p. 16
New image making, pp. 23–29
Shape and form, pp. 58–63

Articulated forms based on an apple, upper left and lower, and on a yellow squash, upper right.

Textured Line Imprint

Task:

Develop a composition of textured lines by using the edge of cardboard or the edge of objects to print the line.

1. Create lines by using small pieces of illustration board or objects with edges that can be painted and then pressed and/or scraped onto the surface to leave an imprinted line.

2. Some lines should touch the edge of the composition. Some lines may end without touching another line. All types of lines may be used: horizontal, vertical, diagonal, curved, and free-formed.

3. Use several hues, varying intensity and value.

Materials:

Paper with a soft surface
Illustration board
Objects with sturdy edges that can be painted and printed
Opaque water-based paint
Brushes

Outcomes:

—Learn to work with informal line and the printing method of producing line quality and variation.
—Increase awareness of texture in line structure.

Text References:

Discussion and examples of line, pp. 35, 36
Discussion and examples of texture, pp. 64–66

A nonobjective composition of textured line and shape.

Brush
Calligraphy

Task:

Create a unified, cohesive nonfigurative line composition to be executed with freehand brush strokes.

1. First practice with watercolor brush and black paint on newsprint. Make at least fifteen trials—some without lifting the brush, and some with two or three lifts. Pressure creates thick line; a light touch gives a thin, delicate line.

2. Select the most successful trial and enlarge it to fill a 9″ × 12″ page.

3. Execute the selected composition in two stages. Paint some of the lines with thin, diluted black. Paint lines to achieve light gray values. Allow to dry. Complete the composition with dense black paint to achieve strong contrasts. Also experiment with a brush loaded with a mixture of diluted black and dense black paint on the brush tip.

Materials:

Newsprint paper and want ad section of newspaper
Medium to large watercolor brush
Black or blue opaque water-based paint

Outcomes:

—Experience the rhythmic flow of spontaneous brush line.
—Understand that practice is necessary to achieve control of brush calligraphy.
—Appreciate the beauty of calligraphy line.

Text References:

Brush calligraphy, p. 32
Expressive textured line, p. 167.

Brush calligraphy showing lines of subtle variation.

Line and Shape Structure

Task:

Design an interconnected line structure with carefully planned accents of black and colored shapes.

1. Draw a series of straight and/or curved lines in space to create an interconnected structure of lines. There should be no loose floating lines, only lines connected as if they were attached to each other by welding. Some of the lines must touch the edge of the composition.

2. Fill in selected spaces defined by the interconnected line structure with black and vivid color to create visual accents. Work for contrast in size and contrast of open space to filled space.

3. Work out the composition on layout paper first and then transfer to illustration board for final rendering.

Outcomes:

—Learn to use variation in line direction, contrasts of vivid color and size relationships in building composition.
—Increase awareness of positive space and negative space.
—Learn the importance of linkage and coordination of line elements in building a cohesive design structure.

Text References:

—Linear continuity and coordination, p. 22
—Interconnected linear structure, p. 37 (upper left)
—Rhythmically connected structure, p. 184
—Line and shape in furniture, p. 176

Materials:

Layout paper and illustration board
Pencil
Brushes (small)
Ruling pen
Straightedge and French curve
Opaque water-based paint and black ink

Structure of interconnected lines and shapes.

Line Contrast
Composition

Task:

Develop a design that contrasts and relates a small organic line composition to a mechanical line structure that surrounds the small composition.

1. Draw a 2½″ × 2½″ square, or a rectangle of similar size in the center of a 10″ × 10″ board. Using a crow-quill pen, create a detailed line drawing of a natural object such as a feather, twig, or leaf with lines that touch all four sides of the small square or rectangle. Use brown ink.

2. Outline the small composition with a black line, using a straightedge and ruling pen.

3. In the area surrounding the small composition, plan a line structure of straight and curved lines by extending selected lines from the crow-quill composition to form a connection between the inner area and the surrounding area. Execute these lines using a ruling pen, straightedge, and French curve. Use black ink for these lines.

Outcomes:

—Learn to experiment with both freehand and mechanical line.
—Increase awareness of organic and structured characteristics of line quality.
—Increase awareness of the relationship of a small defined space in a composition to the whole composition.

Text References:

Organic and mechanical line, p. 34
Freehand line, pp. 38–39
Relationship of small defined space to whole composition p. 42 (lower right), 155 (lower)
Contrast of geometric to organic line, p. 122

Materials:

10″ × 10″ illustration board
Crow-quill pen and ruling pen
Straightedge and French curve
Brown ink and black ink

Line continuity building connections between inner
and outer defined spaces.

Balsa
Linear Cube

Task:

Construct a 12″ × 12″ cube of balsa sticks with interior divisions of space formed by horizontal and vertical members.

1. Construct the 12″ × 12″ linear cube of ¼″ balsa sticks. Careful measurement and a plan for joining the balsa wood at each corner is critical for a well-crafted piece.

2. Sketch and plan the placement of interior units.

3. Construct and link the interior units, and connect them to the basic cube.

4. Design the interior units to create a lively interplay of defined subvolumes.

5. Develop a sense of small- to large-scale proportional relationships.

6. Again, craft is important in making sure that all linear elements are truly horizontal and vertical.

7. As construction proceeds, view the design from varying viewpoints, a special challenge in three-dimensional design.

Materials:

¼″ balsa wood
Exacto-knife or single-edge razor blade
   Warning: Use extreme caution when working with sharp instruments.
Right triangle (90°)
Ruler
Fast-drying model cement

Outcomes:

—Develop a sense of fine proportion in space division.
—Be aware of the interrelationship of parts to the whole, creating a carefully considered asymmetrical balance within the confines of a formal equilateral defined form.
—Pay attention to the importance of craft.

Text References:

Spatial proportion, p. 72
Proportion, pp. 73–75
Asymmetrical balance, pp. 81–82
Proportion in architecture, p. 133
Linear structure in furniture, p. 156 (lower)

An interplay of line and space division in three dimensions.

Line 211

Line and Shape Construction

Task:

Construct a three-dimensional form made up of line and shape.

1. The structure should be designed as an interplay of line using wire or light rods. This is one way of three-dimensional form-building, using the additive process.

2. Within the linear structure, plan a series of similar flat shapes made of thin metal. These shapes appear to be visually caught in space within the confines of the wire lines.

3. Begin the project by sketching ideas on paper to determine the linear structure and the number, size, and similar outlines of the shapes to be used. While the scale of the shapes may vary considerably, the outline of the shapes should be similar. The repeat of similar shapes will contribute to the unity of the project.

4. Use light metal rods or wires that can be easily soldered to each other or to the thin metal shapes. Be sure the metals are compatible and can be soldered with a simple soldering iron.

5. Consider the color and texture of the metal carefully. Consider the visual weight of the shapes to the weight of the wire structure. Turn the project often as you work. Remember that the viewer has the option of walking around the piece and viewing it from 360°.

6. The structure may be designed to stand on its own form, or it may be anchored to a simple wooden base.

Materials:

Wire rod and/or wire
Flat thin metal sheet material
Solder and flux and soldering iron
Warning: Use extreme caution when working with the hot soldering iron. Use solder and flux that is free of cadmium, lead and fluoride.
Wire cutters, metal shears, and needle-nose pliers
Pencil and paper
Patina solution

Outcomes:

—Learn to control both linear and shape elements in three dimensions.
—Increase awareness of space captured within an open form.
—Increase awareness of form-building by the additive process.

Text References:

Observation of line, p. 35
Shape into form, p. 61

Three-dimensional structures composed of line and shape.

Line

213

Black and Gray Squares

Task:

Create a balanced, coordinated composition based on black and gray squares.

1. Use 8″ × 10″ middle-value gray construction paper as background. Measure and cut seven 1″ black construction paper squares and five ½″ dark gray squares.

2. Arrange seven black squares and five gray squares on middle-value gray ground. Goals:
   a. Work for linear coordination and continuity— awareness of edges.
   b. Be aware of balance—feel the weight of the black squares.
   c. Avoid predictable sequences—i.e., stairsteps.
   d. Design the spaces between squares—avoid monotonous intervals.
   e. Position all squares parallel to boundaries of the background—avoid any tilting.

3. Move, shift, and arrange critically the twelve given squares until all above goals are reached. Stand away from your work and view it objectively.

4. Adhere arranged squares to background.

5. Variation: increase the number of squares and add a black-and-white 1″ magazine illustration, cut out in such a way as to obscure the objects pictured.

6. Variation: using a large magazine illustration, cut and arrange squares so that the inner movement of the original illustration is retained.

Materials:

Black and gray construction paper
Exacto-knife or scissors
   Warning: Use extreme caution when working with sharp instruments.
Triangle and straightedge
Glue

Outcomes:

—Develop an awareness of the line-coordinating function of edge alignment by avoiding tilted and haphazard positioning.
—Become aware of the function of continuity, movement, flow, and spacing in creating a unified design.
—Refine the sense of visual balance.

Text References:

Edge coordination and balance, p. 82 (upper)
Edge alignment, p. 84 (lower right)

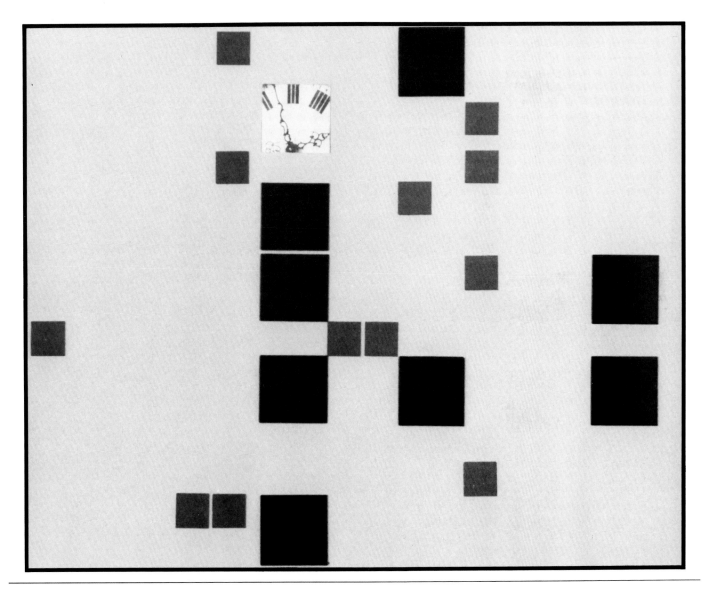

Black and gray squares with collage square for emphasis.

Value

215

Line and Value Structure

Task:

Develop a three-stage assignment starting with a black vertical and horizontal line structure on white ground. Translate into a dark- and light-value composition based on the original line structure. Finally, develop a more subtle value composition on a framework that is a diagonal interpretation of the original line structure.

1. On a white ground, create an 8″ × 10″ nonfigurative composition strictly limited to vertical, horizontal lines that may move from top to bottom, and horizontal lines that move from left to right, lines may be interrupted at selected points (e.g., where a vertical intersects a horizontal).

    a. Make use of three or four different thicknesses of line, varying from hairline to 2″.
    b. Try four or five thumbnail sketches of varying ideas until a balanced, well spaced composition results.
    c. Enlarge and perfect your best design.
    d. Render in black ink using a ruling pen and black paint.
    e. Strong value contrast will result.

2. Using the same composition, make most of the lines disappear by translating all resulting shapes into values of neutral gray. Execute or render in paint.

3. Next, vary the strict vertical/horizontal composition by tilting both horizontal and vertical lines until an informal, playful, eccentric composition results. Render this composition in *one* hue, using many subtle values.

Materials:

White paper or illustration board
India ink and opaque water-based paint
Ruling pen and brushes
Straightedge

Outcomes:

—Learn to use both strong, sharp value contrast as well as subtle value relationships.
—Develop visual judgment in spacing decisions and proportional choices.
—Learn to expand upon and refine basic ideas.

Text References:

Positive/negative space relationships, p. 70
Proportion, pp. 72–75
Use of value in textile design, p. 169 (upper)
High contrast of value, p. 170

Three variations of line and value to build composition.

Value

217

Cube Structure
in Black and Grays

Task:

Construct a cube structure made up of at least eight cubes of different sizes and different values of gray.

1. Begin the project by sketching ideas on paper using informal perspective to suggest depth in arranging eight to ten cubes. Use the idea of cantilever as well as the principle of asymmetrical balance.

2. Determine the size of the largest cube (probably no more than 6") and construct it of illustration board, carefully cut and glued.

3. Construct additional cubes that are scaled to size relative to the large cube, using the sketch as a guide.

4. Begin the assembly of cubes by using masking tape to hold the cubes in place as you adjust and readjust them. Turn the structure to view it from all sides.

5. When all design decisions are complete, glue cubes together by carefully removing sections of tape, gluing and retaping to hold the pieces together until the glue is dry. It may not be possible to glue all the cubes together at one time.

6. Sand edges lightly and paint the cubes with a white undercoat. Resand. Select values of gray, mix, and paint individual cubes. Use value to add to the drama of the structure.

7. Spray the project with a mat finish to protect the surface. *Spray in a well ventilated area and use a mask.*

Materials:

Illustration board and drawing paper
Mat knife and straightedge
   Warning: Use extreme caution when working with sharp instruments.
Masking tape and glue
Opaque water-based paint
Brush
Sandpaper
Matte spray

Outcomes:

—Increase awareness of interrelation of unit to unit, and the importance of each unit to the whole.
—Learn to work with mass and the flow of space to create total volume.
—Learn to work with both physical balance and visual balance.

Text References:

Use of gray by Albers, p. 161
Discussion of shape and form, p. 58
Modulation of value, p. 41

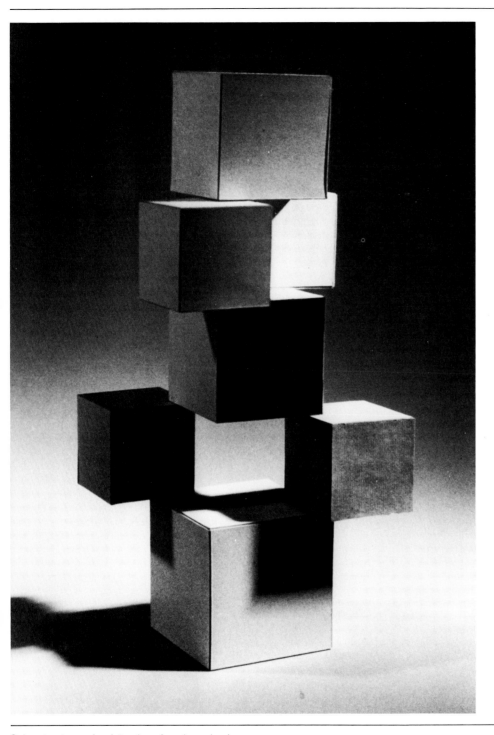

Cube structure using interplay of scale and value.

Value 219

Value and Intensity Chart

Task:

Construct a value and intensity chart from painted swatches.

1. Grid a large piece of paper into at least forty rectangular shapes, 1½″ × 3″. In a palette or small dish, place a large puddle of white paint. Add a drop of black pigment, mix, and paint an even swatch in the first rectangle. Continue the process of adding black, mixing, and painting in each successive rectangle until near-black is reached.

2. Cut the rectangular shapes apart and select the best range of nine evenly spaced values from the near-white value to the near-black value. Cut the selected nine values to 1″ × 2″ rectangles and glue to a gray board with ⅛″ between the rectangles. Near-black is at the base and near-white is the top of the scale. The gray value scale is complete.

3. Select a hue, paint a flat swatch, and match it to the one value on the gray scale that is closest. To make a matching nine-step value scale for the selected hue, add white to the pure hue to create the lighter values, and add black to the pure hue to create the darker values. Try to match the hue value scale step-by-step to the value steps of the gray scale. Cut the nine values to 1″ × 2″ rectangles and glue to the board, leaving ⅛″ between rectangles and ¼″ between the gray scale and the hue value scale.

4. Select a pair of complementary hues for the intensity chart. Start with a puddle of one of the hues and paint the first swatch. Add a drop of the complementary hue, mix, and paint a swatch. Continue the process until the mixture turns a neutral gray. Repeat the process, starting with the other complement as base hue. Select four equally spaced steps from full intensity to near-neutral for both of the complementary hues. Cut to 1″ × 2″ rectangles and arrange into a horizontal scale with full intensity on the outside moving to neutral gray in the center. Display the intensity scale of eight steps at the base of the value scales.

Materials:

Gray mat board (10″ × 15″)
Large white paper
Opaque water-based paint
Flat brush
Exacto-knife and straightedge
  Warning: Use extreme caution when working with sharp instruments.
Glue

Outcomes:

—Learn to manipulate value and intensity in paint.
—Increase awareness of the full range of hue, value, and intensity.

Text References:

Discussion and examples of color, pp. 44–51

LIGHTER NEXT TO WHITE	LIGHTER NEXT TO WHITE
LIGHTER ADD WHITE	LIGHTER ADD WHITE
LIGHTER ADD WHITE	LIGHTER ADD WHITE
LIGHTER ADD WHITE	LIGHTER ADD WHITE
LIGHTER ADD WHITE	MIDDLE VALUE
PURE BLUE NATURAL VALUE	DARKER ADD BLACK
DARKER ADD BLACK	DARKER ADD BLACK
DARKER ADD BLACK	DARKER ADD BLACK
DARKER NEXT TO BLACK	DARKER NEXT TO BLACK

ORANGE — DULLER ADD BLUE — DULLER ADD BLUE — DULLER ADD BLUE — DULLER ADD ORANGE — DULLER ADD ORANGE — DULLER ADD ORANGE — BLUE

Blueprint for value and intensity chart.

Color

221

Colorful Squares

Task:

Create a series of nonobjective color compositions using six different color harmonies.

1. Make a series of grid structures of horizontal and vertical lines in a 4″ square that create six to fifteen areas for color.

2. Using colored papers and colored areas from magazines, cut shapes to fit the grid structures. By using all three color properties (hue, value, and chroma), create color compositions which demonstrate:
   a. monochromatic harmony (p. 52 in text)
   b. complementary harmony (p. 52 in text)
   c. analogous harmony (p. 53 in text)
   d. contrast of dark/light (p. 55 in text)
   e. contrast of warm/cool (p. 55 in text)
   f. contrast of bright/dull (p. 56 in text)

3. Select one composition and enlarge it to a 15″ × 15″ board. Using opaque water-based paint and masking tape, translate the small composition into a painted composition. Tape edges of the area to be painted and apply paint with a flat brush, as evenly as possible. When paint is dry, remove tape. Retape for the next area, and paint. Be sure paint is dry each time, and carefully remove tape each time, in order not to harm the surface of the painted areas.

Materials:

Illustration board and colored papers
Magazines
Exacto-knife and straightedge
   Warning: Use extreme caution when working with sharp instruments.
Opaque water-based paint
Flat brush
Masking tape

Outcomes:

—Learn to create basic color compositions with cut papers and with paint.
—Increase awareness of the rich potential of the three properties of color.

Text References:

Discussion and examples of color harmony, pp. 52–57

Color harmonies—see text for color examples.

Collage Paint Match

Task:

Create a nonfigurative textural composition comprised of torn and cut paper. Translate the composition into painted form.

1. Tear and cut shapes from colored paper and magazines, and arrange them in a composition so that positive and negative areas are easily seen.

2. Arrange cut and torn shapes, and glue onto a 7″ × 10″ board.

3. Place a piece of tracing paper over the composition and draw a 1″ grid over the entire composition.

4. Draw a light 2″ grid on a 14″ × 20″ illustration board, and, using the grid as a guide, transfer the composition onto the illustration board.

5. Match the colors of the collage and paint the composition, being careful to maintain the textural quality of the paper collage.

Materials:

Colored papers and magazine collage materials
Tracing paper and illustration board
Opaque water-based paint and brushes
Exacto-knife and scissors
 Warning: Use extreme caution when working with sharp instruments.
Glue

Outcomes:

—Learn to match any color and to translate a small composition to a large composition.
—Increase awareness of design elements in building a free form, nonfigurative composition.

Text References:

Discussion of shape, pp. 58–63
Discussion of color, pp. 48–51

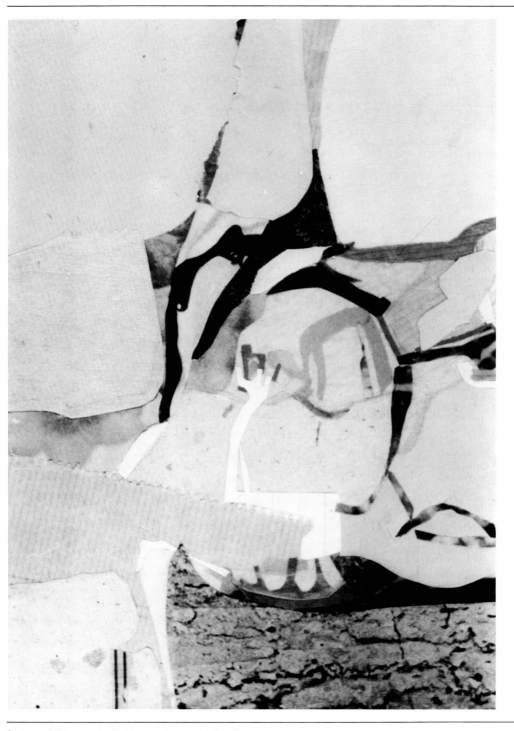

Color matching—a test of hue, value, and intensity
understanding and skill.

Outline and Solid Shapes

Task:

Create a composition of open (outlined) shapes and closed (filled-in) shapes.

1. Using thin ink lines, draw four or five overlapping circles of varying sizes. Select several of the shapes created by the overlap and ink in as solid shapes. Select to achieve a dynamic balance between open and closed shapes. Plan to have the open shapes dominant and the filled-in areas subordinate.

2. Using thin ink lines, draw five to seven rectangles that overlap one another. Select and ink in shapes created by the overlap.

3. Repeat the same process using triangular shapes.

4. With a soft pencil, draw a series of curving lines that intersect. Create a rhythmic sweep by moving the pencil in a free and spontaneous spirit. Examine the resulting drawing, and select a number of shapes to fill in to create emphasis and balance based on dominance and subordination.

Outcomes:

—Develop an awareness of outline and solid shape in building composition.
—Practice the selection process in making critical design decisions.
—Develop sensitivity to the principles of balance, subordination, and emphasis.

Text References:

Contrast of positive and negative shapes, p. 22
Fortuitous shapes, p. 37 (upper left)
Shape and form, pp. 58–63
Relation of positive and negative shapes, p. 95 (upper)
Interlocking shapes, p. 166 (upper)
Interplay of line and shape, p. 184

Materials:

Fine-tip ink pen and inking compass
Soft lead pencil
Smooth surface paper or board
Drawing paper
Black ink

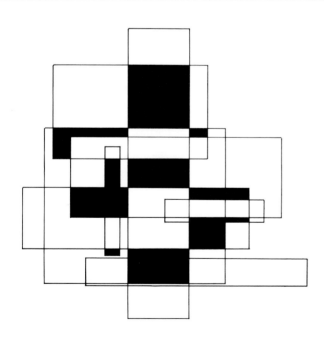

An interplay of overlapping shapes—open and closed.

Angular Shape Structure

Task:

Construct a nonobjective composition based on horizontal and diagonal lines which define positive and negative angular shapes.

1. Adhere pressure-sensitive paper to the surface of illustration board.

2. With an exacto-knife and straightedge, lightly cut twenty parallel straight horizontal lines across the paper. Vary intervals between lines.

3. Cut ten diagonal lines of varying lengths, starting and stopping the diagonal cuts at selected horizontal lines. Vary the length of these diagonal lines and angle some of the lines to the left and some to the right.

4. Now look at the shapes defined by these cut lines and select shapes to peel off, thereby exposing the white board. The result will be an active interplay of positive and negative angular shapes.

5. Be aware of the continuity of edge alignment and contrasts of large to small areas and variety in shape outline.

Materials:

7" × 11" pressure-sensitive paper of any color
Illustration board
Exacto-knife and straightedge
   Warning: Use extreme caution when working with sharp instruments.

Outcomes:

—Learn to control composition by combining with both positive and negative shapes.
—Increase awareness of interval, movement, and balance in building composition.

Text References:

Discussion and examples of shape, pp. 58–60
Positive/negative space relationships, p. 70
Interaction of positive and negative space, p. 179 (upper)

An active interplay between positive and negative shapes.

Metamorphosis

Task:

Create a six-step metamorphosis that gradually changes a selected organic shape into a selected geometric shape.

1. Using a 3″-square finder, look through magazines and trace a single flat organic shape and a geometric shape. The resulting single shapes may well encompass several objects or parts of objects. (Note the organic shape on the opposite page surrounds three leaves, a flower, and a piece of driftwood.)

2. Using rough working drawings on tracing paper, develop four intermediate steps to bring about the visual transformation from organic to geometric.

3. using tracing paper overlays, change, refine, and adjust the images to create a step-by-step gradual metamorphosis.

4. When the refinement is complete, transfer the six designs to six 3″ × 3″ illustration boards. Render each design in black paint.

5. Finally, arrange the six squares in two rows, starting with the organic design in the upper left square and ending with the geometric design in the lower right square.

Materials:

Magazines
Tracing paper and illustration board
Scissors and exacto-knife
  Warning: Use extreme caution when working with sharp instruments.
Ruling pen and brush
Straightedge
Black paint
Glue

Outcomes:

—Discover the visual attributes that characterize organic and geometric shape.
—Understand the idea of metamorphosis and how to pace visual change.
—Work for refinement of ideas, and learn to extend and change beginning ideas into a carefully developed design.

Text References:

Transition from shape to form, p. 61
Metamorphosis of image, p. 70

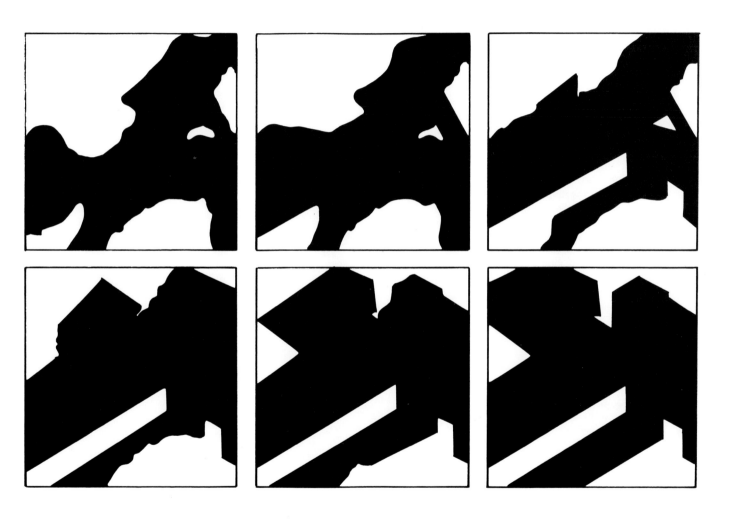

Metamorphosis: a transition from an organic shape to a geometric shape.

Contrast Collage

Task:

Design a collage which combines very precise geometric shapes and contrasting irregular torn shapes.

1. Arrange a selected number of geometric shapes cut from collage material.

2. Weave torn shapes over, around, and under the geometric shapes.

3. Through color, texture, and line relationships, create a unified composition of contrasting forms. Although sharply contrasting forms seem incompatible, it takes design judgment to create a sense of unity. Use only magazine advertisement collage material and completely cover a 9″ × 12″ surface.

4. Experiment with a variety of possible solutions before adhering the collage material to the board.

Materials:

Magazine collage
Mat board
Scissors and exacto-knife
   Warning: Use extreme caution when working with sharp instruments.
Glue

Outcomes:

—Understand the inherent nature of precise shapes and the contrasting freedom of irregular shapes.
—Learn to harmonize contrasting shapes by controlling other visual elements, i.e., color, texture, value, and line, to create unity.
—Learn to use judicious manipulation and trial and error in building composition.

Text References:

Discussion and examples of shape, pp. 58–63
Contrast of geometric and organic shape, p. 122
Contrast of geometric and figurative shape, p. 126

A composition based on geometric shapes and torn
irregular shapes.

Radial Bas Relief

Task:

Create a 10″ square paper relief, radial in design, comprised of four to six similar forms.

1. In pencil, sketch a basic radial design on newsprint paper, indicating shapes, arrangement, and rough suggestions of relief.

2. Select a substantial colored or white paper and translate the largest drawn shape into an actual three-dimensional form. Construct it out of a single piece of paper by cutting, scoring, and gluing. Plan for tabs to hold the form together and a flat surface that will be used to attach the form to a background.

3. Create a paper pattern for each different size and shape to facilitate the construction of duplicate forms.

4. Assemble the several constructed components, making final adjustments.

5. Adhere all forms to a flat sheet of the same selected paper which has been glued to cardboard for stability.

Materials:

Sketch paper, pencil
Selected substantial paper (heavy enough for scoring and folding)
Exacto-knife
   Warning: Use extreme caution when working with sharp instruments.
Glue
Straightedge
Cardboard

Outcomes:

—Develop an understanding of modular and radial design.
—Experience the translation of a two-dimensional sketch into a three-dimensional relief.

Text References:

Radial balance, p. 82 (lower)
Radial design, pp. 85 (upper), 96 (upper and lower right)
The sun symbol as radial design, p. 104

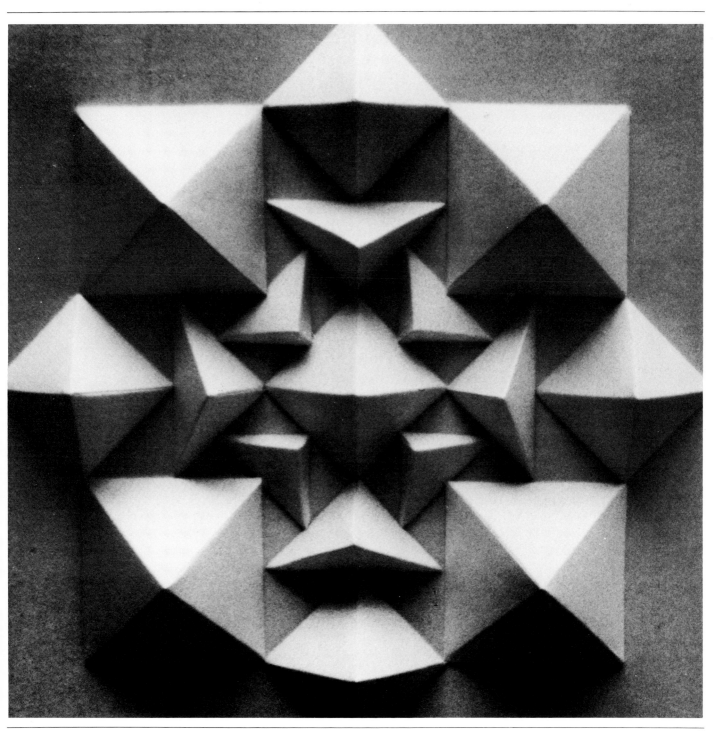

Bas-relief—a transition of flat shapes to three-dimensional form.

Shape and Form

Cube Surface Design

Task:

Construct a cardboard cube with a design that is repeated on all six sides of the cube.

1. Draw a 4″ × 4″ square. Develop a design that touches the edge of the square at several points.

2. Trace the design onto tracing paper two times and place the squares next to each other; observe how the design interconnects. Experiment with two squares side by side using a mirror image, an upside-down image, a rotated image, or a split image.

3. Trace the design on an additional square and tape all three squares together to form the three sides of a cube. Observe what happens to the design as it connects on three sides. If the design does not interconnect to create a ready flow or a transition from side to side, adjust and refine the basic design so that elements connect.

4. Carefully cut out six square shapes. If you use a bevel cut, all six sides will be equal. If you use a straight cut, determine how the box will be glued and account for the thickness of the cardboard as you cut side pieces and bottom and top pieces.

5. Glue the box and paint it with a white undercoat. Sand lightly if necessary. Transfer the design to all six sides and paint. You may want to spray the project with a mat finish to protect the surface. *Spray in a well ventilated area and use a face mask.*

Materials:

Illustration board and tracing paper
Mat knife and straightedge
   Warning: Use extreme caution when working with sharp instruments.
Masking tape and glue
Sand paper
Opaque water-based paint
Brush
Mat spray

Outcomes:

—Develop a sense of craft.
—Discover what happens to the surface design as it wraps around a three-dimensional volume.
—Increase awareness of how surface design affects three-dimensional form.

Text References:

Discussion of shape and form, pp. 58–63
Surface design on form, pp. 95 (upper), 97 (lower left), 102

Surface design adjusted and fitted to the six sides of
each cube.

Monolithic Form

Task:

Create a monolithic solid form incorporating both convex and concave elements.

1. Begin the project by sketching with a pencil, attempting to describe a solid form which has both convex and concave areas. Think of the surrounding space as moving around and into the surface but without completely penetrating the form.

2. Mix a thick plaster solution and pour it into a cut-off half-gallon milk carton or a similar cardboard container that can be cut away when the plaster is set.

3. When the plaster is just set (it may still have a slightly warm feel to the touch), peel away the carton. With a knife or other plaster tool, carefully cut away excess plaster to the rough structure of the planned piece. At this stage the plaster will cut easily, so care must be exercised to cut away only the large unwanted areas. When the plaster is hard, more detailed and careful carving can be executed to reveal the desired form.

4. Final rasping and sanding will be necessary to finish the final form. If very smooth surfaces are desired, several sandings, using coarse, fine, and extra fine sandpaper, will be necessary. The sketch will be the guide toward which to work, but careful adjustments may be desirable as the piece is developed and can be viewed from all sides.

Materials:

Plaster of paris
Mixing container
Milk carton or other carton
Knife or other plaster carving tools
Rasp
   Warning: Use extreme caution when working with sharp instruments.
Sand paper.

Outcomes:

—Experience the subtractive method of carving form out of a solid mass.
—Increase awareness of solid form and the flow of space over and around the surface of the form.
—Work to control transition of concave and convex areas.
—Be aware of light and shadow on the surface of a solid.

Text References:

From shape to form, p. 61
Form modulation, p. 63
Transitions within a single form, p. 65
Functional form, pp. 163, 165

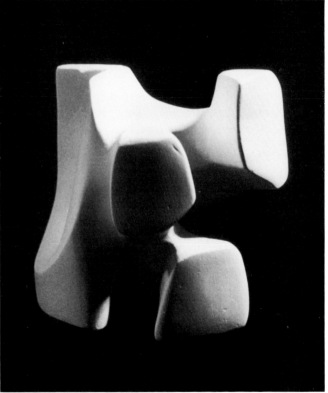

Monolithic forms carved out of solid masses.

Texture Samples

Task:

Create a series of invented texture samples.

1. Develop twenty-five small 1″ × 2½″; twenty-five medium 2″ × 3⅓″; and twenty-five large 3″ × 4″ texture experiments.

2. Produce these areas using a mixture of:
   a. water-based paint
   b. wax crayon
   c. colored inks, including black and sepia
   d. white glue

3. Make six or eight of each of the following:
   a. Start with a first layer of wax crayon, varying hue and pressure. Add a layer of ink which will penetrate the wax only partially. If ink coating is too dense, allow ink to dry—rub, crumple, or scrape to induce texture.
   b. Next, paint six different samples, using six different hues. Allow to dry and add layer of contrasting wax crayon. Watch for and induce interesting color interplay. If wax coating is too heavy, some of it may be scraped off.
   c. This time, coat paper with ink first, then add layers of both wax and paint.
   d. Using wax crayon, make six rubbings of available textured surfaces: wood, cement, plaster, vinyl, and leather.
   e. Pat, sponge, or scrape glue, and allow to dry. Apply ink, crayon, or paint onto dried glue surface, etc. Modify some by adding a wash of paint and/or ink.

4. Select the best twelve to fifteen; crop and arrange as squares and/or rectangles on a neutral or white ground, creating a coordinated, planned composition.

Materials:

Opaque water-based paint
Wax crayon
Colored inks, including black and sepia
Glue
Brushes and scraping tool
Illustration board

Outcomes:

—Expand textural awareness and ability to invent textures.
—Encourage experimentation with a variety of materials.
—Exercise visual selection and critical judgment.

Text References:

Discussion and examples of texture, pp. 64–68
Invented texture, pp. 67, 68 (upper)
Descriptive object texture, p. 93

Texture and Pattern

A series of invented textures.

Texture Composition

Task:

Create a nonfigurative collage of paper and printed textures on an invented texture background.

1. Select the best single invented texture sample (from previous project) for the background texture.

2. On stretched drawing paper 12″ × 14″, recreate the selected texture, enlarging it until it fills the entire surface. Do not allow the background to become too active. Use close value contrast.

3. Using a variety of textured paper (e.g., brown-bag paper, tissue, magazine printed textures, etc.) create a series of touching and interlocking shapes, combining straight, diagonal, and curved-line nonfigurative shapes to create a unified, rhythmic design.

4. Allow at least one-third of your textured ground to show.

5. Paying close attention to textural contrasts and textural scale, allow some shapes to create little contrast, others to contrast greatly with the background.

6. Adhere shapes to textured ground.

Materials:

Wax crayon, paint, inks, glue
Scissors and exacto-knife
   Warning: Use extreme caution when working with sharp instruments.
Brushes
Drawing paper
Butcher tape
Tracing paper
Drawing pencil

Outcome:

—Develop sensitivity to scale, color, and value of textures.
—Exercise imaginative powers in creating a nonfigurative design.

Text References:

Discussion and examples of texture, pp. 64–68

A nonfigurative composition emphasizing texture.

Rhythmic Pattern

Task:

Using single or multiple motifs, create a rhythmic repeat pattern.

1. Choose a basic, two-dimensional shape and repeat it, utilizing only regular recurrence. Render in black ink, or cut black paper on white drawing paper.

2. Combine two basic shapes, alternating in recurrence. Render in black ink, or black paper on white drawing paper.

3. Overlap the two basic shapes chosen and invert the dark/light. Render as in #1 and #2.

4. On a 12″ × 12″ square, divide the entire area into 2″ squares. Using two contrasting hues, alternate one dark, one light. On each square, place a circle or half circle of contrasting hue—light circle against dark squares, dark circle against light squares. Adhere all units with glue or rubber cement.

5. Create a second 12″ × 12″ dark/light background grid, using a different pair of hues. Against the grid, invent one or two motifs and proceed to alternate dark hue, light hue, to create contrast.

Materials:

White drawing paper, illustration board, origami paper
India ink
Ruling pen and brush
White glue, rubber cement
Scissors, exacto-knife
   Warning: Use extreme caution when working with sharp instruments.
Compass

Outcomes:

—Develop an awareness of the basic methods of creating pattern.
—See the rhythmic repeat of selected motifs as visual enrichment.
—Exercise invention and imagination.
—Sharpen hue and value skills.

Text References:

Natural pattern, pp. 13, 17
Surface pattern, pp. 30 (upper left), 31 (lower)
Textile pattern, pp. 57 (lower left), 185
Use of alternation and inversion of motif, p. 68 (lower)
Types of repetition, pp. 84, 85

Texture and Pattern

A pattern based on a connecting motif.

Word Pattern

Task:

Create a pattern by repeating a word or name at least six to twelve times.

1. Experiment first with thumbnail trials in soft drawing pencil until the repeat pattern is developed.

    a. Stretch and distort selected letters.
    b. Compress and squeeze selected letters.
    c. The stretching and compression should empha-size the geometric character of the letters. Success is achieved when the resulting geometric pattern is perceived *first* and the word *last*.

2. Use upper-case, single-stroke letters formed by a round-nibbed speedball pen and black india ink.

3. Execute the refined pattern on a full sheet of daily newspaper want ad page. Use the columns horizontally as a guide for the inked letters.

4. Experiment further with lower-case letter forms.

Materials:

Soft drawing pencil
News stock for preliminary sketches
Black india ink
Round-nib speedball pen
Want ad section of daily newspaper

Outcomes:

—Develop a playful, inventive use of a selected word or name.
—Explore the geometric possibilities of letter forms to create imaginative pattern.
—Understand that altering the proportions of letter forms can create a lively and unique pattern.

Text References:

Repetition of motif, pp. 83–85
Letter repetition, p. 180 (upper)

A pattern based on letter form manipulation.

Positive to Negative Transformation

Task:

Create a nonfigurative mirror image on a white ground from shapes cut out of a black ground. To create a gradual transition from black to white, cut many shapes at or near the center tangent edges of the black and white grounds, and gradually diminish size and/or number of cut-out shapes as the design evolves outward from the center axis.

1. Geometric transformation

   a. Cut two rectangles 6½″ × 4½″—one white, one black—and place them tangent to each other, end to end.
   b. Starting at the edge of the black piece that is tangent to the white, cut geometric shapes decreasing in number as the design moves away from the center axis.
   c. Place each cut black shape in a mirror arrangement on the white ground.
   d. After cutting and arranging is completed, glue the shapes and mount the rectangles onto a white mat board.

2. Freeform transformation

   a. Start with two tangent black and white rectangles.
   b. Repeat process, cutting irregular and informal shapes.

Materials:

White and black construction paper
Mat board
Exacto-knife
   Warning: Use extreme caution when working with sharp instruments.
Glue
Straightedge

Outcomes:

—Learn to control and create a transition of positive to negative shapes.
—Understand the importance of economy of means, making full and efficient use of each cut shape.
—See the relationship of sharply contrasting positive to negative and negative to positive shapes.

Text References:

Transition from negative to positive, pp. 59, 84
Positive to negative relationship, p. 109 (lower left)

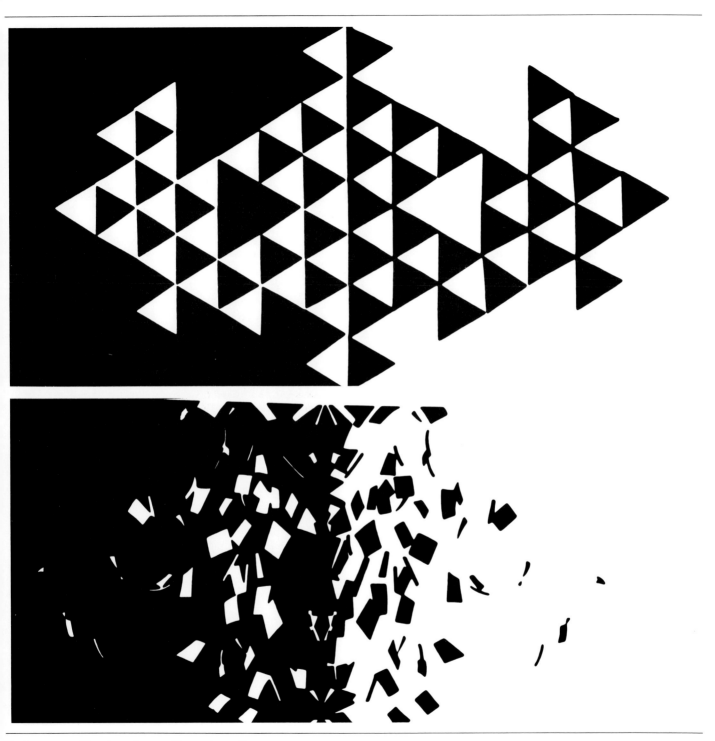

Design compositions based on positive and negative shapes.

Space
249

Space Collage

Task:

Create, with magazine collage material, an imaginative design that not only leads the eye vertically and horizontally, but also into pictorial illusionary space.

1. Select images of any subject of your choice, either figurative or nonfigurative.

2. Cut images along their contours.

3. By using relative size, receding lines, advancing and receding values, develop the illusion of pictorial space. Reinforce the space illusion with color passages that move forward and color passages that melt into the background. Work to create a visual sense of foreground, middle ground, and background.

4. Experiment with a number of possible solutions before adhering the collage material to an 8″ × 10″ board.

Outcomes:

—Increase awareness of the advancing and receding qualities of values and colors that help to create an illusion of pictorial space.
—Learn to experiment with the illusion of space in creating foreground, middle ground, and background space.
—Learn to use size and linear perspective to create the illusion of deep space.

Text References:

Discussion and examples of the illusion of space, p. 71
Space recession, p. 72
Pictorial space, p. 93

Materials:

Magazines
Illustration or mat board
Scissors and exacto-knife
Warning: Use extreme caution when working with sharp instruments.
Glue

Compositions based on the illusion of deep space and
shallow space.

Proportion: Exercises in Visual Relationships

Task:

Create in nonfigurative line a series of space division exercises that demonstrate variety in proportion and interval.

1. In an 8″ × 10″ rectangle positioned vertically, arrange seven horizontal lines of equal thickness.

2. Repeat above assignment, using nine horizontal lines of equal thickness.

3. Repeat above assignment, using fourteen horizontal lines of equal thickness.

4. In an 8″ × 10″ rectangle, arrange four vertical lines of three different thicknesses.

5. In an 8″ × 10″ rectangle, arrange six vertical lines of four different thicknesses.

6. In an 8″ × 10″ rectangle, arrange seven vertical lines of six different thicknesses.

Allow all vertical and horizontal lines in the above exercises to extend the full length and width of the rectangle.

Materials:

8″ × 10″ white drawing paper
India ink, felt-nib pen, or ruling pen
Straightedge

Outcomes:

—Increase awareness of spacing variety and interval size.
—Learn to see and control both positive (line) and negative (spacing interval) space.
—Sharpen the sense of alertness to proportional diversity and uneven interval.
—Learn the difference between merely putting line down on paper and placing line—or shape, or color, or value.

Text References:

Discussion and examples, pp. 72–75

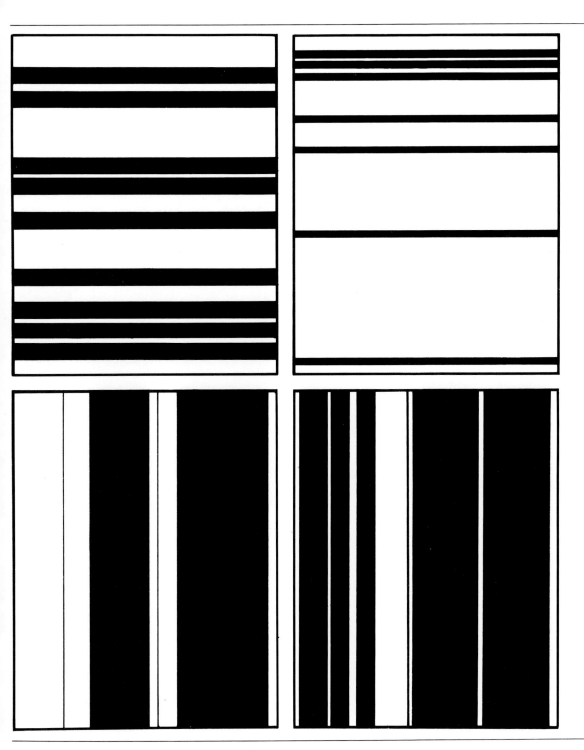

Proportion and interval experiments.

Emphasis

Task:

Design four examples of emphasis in 6″ × 6″ square formats using cut-out shapes or ruled pen lines.

1. Develop visual importance through the use of contrast and incongruity of simple elements such as: size, interval, dark and light, texture, or placement.

2. Work out initial ideas in thumbnail sketches.

3. Lightly trace key guide lines to the illustration board and complete the assignment in ruled pen lines and/or cut-out shapes.

4. Careful use of value and hue will dramatically affect the power of emphasis.

5. By using a full range of value and hue, primary and secondary emphasis areas may be developed.

Materials:

White drawing paper, sketch paper
Colored papers and magazine collage
Opaque water-based paint
Ruling pen and brush
Glue

Outcomes:

—Develop awareness of different visual means of creating emphasis as well as subordination.
—Learn to direct the viewer's attention to selected parts of a design.
—Understand the role of visual emphasis in creating dominance and subordination.

Text References:

Discussion and examples, pp. 76, 77

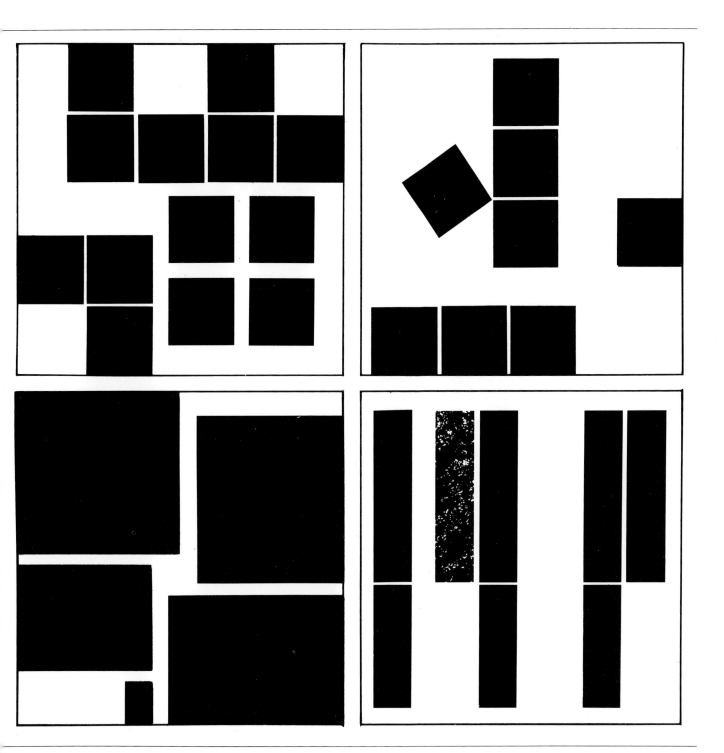

Compositions with an emphasis element.

Movement

Task:

Create different types of implied movement. In 6″ squares, using pen and ink or felt-tip pen, experiment with lines and shapes to create the following types of movement.

1. Rhythmic movement suggested by repeated lines or shapes.

2. Sequential action suggested by slight successive changes in position recording a path of movement.

3. Linear movement that suggests implied force.

4. Linear movement that suggests a path or direction across the surface or leads the eye into illusionary space.

5. An energetic interplay of contrasting movements.

Materials:

White drawing paper
India ink, pen, ruling pen, felt-tip pen
French curve
Brush

Outcomes:

—Develop a sense of design vitality through a variety of line movements.
—Discover the potential of movement on an essentially stationary surface.
—Learn to attract and lead the eye rhythmically across and through a designed image.

Text References:

Discussion and examples, pp. 78–79
Lively suggested movement, p. 90
Undulatory movement, p. 155 (upper)
Flowing and rhythmic movement, pp. 150, 158

Experiments in path and suggested movement.

Balance

Task:

Design three examples of visual balance.

On 8″ × 10″ white paper, using black ink pen or black construction paper, create the following, combining both line and shape.

1. A symmetrical, or formal, balanced composition.

2. An asymmetrical, or informal, composition.

3. A radial balanced composition.

Materials:

White drawing paper
India ink
Ruling pen, felt-nib pen
Brush
Black construction paper
Ruler
Scissors

Outcomes:

—Learn to experience and think in terms of visual balance.
—Create three different forms of visual balance.
—Develop a sensitivity to visual weights, and play these one against the other until a visual equilibrium is achieved.

Text References:

Discussion and examples, pp. 80–82
Formal balance in functional design, pp. 99 (upper), 103

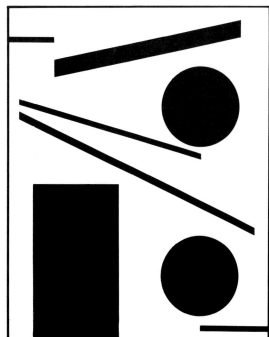

Compositions in formal, radial, and informal balance.

Interaction and Order

Repetition

Task:

Design an example of each of the five basic kinds of repetition.

1. On 6″ × 6″ white drawing paper, create the following in black line and black shapes.
   a. Select a simple geometric shape and repeat it in regularly spaced sequence. Make the chosen motif small enough to be repeated at least eight times horizontally and eight times vertically (64 repeats).
   b. Select two different geometric shapes and alternate the repeat.
   c. Using the two motifs chosen for exercise b, invert and alternate the dark/light of the motifs.
   d. Create an irregular, asymmetrical repeat of one selected geometric motif.
   e. Create a radial repeat of two or three motifs. (This exercise may be executed by folding and cutting with scissors or exacto-knife.)

2. These exercises may be executed with ruling pen and india ink, or they may be printed with an art-gum eraser or a sturdy vegetable cut to the desired shape.

Materials:

White and black drawing paper
India ink
Ruling pen and/or felt-nib pen
Straightedge
Brush
Scissors and exacto-knife
  Warning: Use extreme caution when working with sharp instruments.
Art-gum eraser

Outcomes:

—Learn to organize the motifs in a variety of ways to create visual order through repetition.
—Experience the vitality of visual rhythms.

Text References:

Positive and negative repeat motif, p. 59
Open/closed and inverted motif, p. 68 (lower)
Repetition discussion and examples, pp. 83, 84, 85
Incised geometric pattern, p. 94
Single element repetition, p. 100

Repetition based on geometric shape and dark and light alternation.

Leaf Collage

Task:

Create a collage of dried natural leaves.

1. Collect a variety of dried or partially dried leaves.

2. Dampen and press to flatten.

3. Arrange leaves in a composition using overlays, tangency, vertical and/or horizontal placement. Avoid imitating natural leaf growth patterns and adjust and readjust until a satisfactory design is achieved.

4. When all refinements are complete, adhere leaves to background. Glue into position, using glue liberally on the backs of the leaves.

5. Cover with wax paper and place under a drawing board weighted with books. Press overnight.

Materials:

A collection of leaves
Neutral color mat board of medium to dark value
White glue
Drawing board
Wax paper

Outcomes:

—Develop an alertness to leaf color, shape, line, and texture.
—Practice pure vision.
—Learn to respond to shapes, textures, and axis of leaves as compositional decisions are made.

Text References:

Visual research, pp. 9–21

Compositions using natural materials.

Letter Form Collage

Task:

Create a collage composition of letter forms.

1. Cut lines of print from either magazines or newspapers.
   a. Smallest print size: cut many long, medium, and short lines. Cut to obscure the sentence meanings.
   b. Medium small size: Cut many long, medium, and short lines. Cut to obscure the sentence meanings.
   c. Medium size: Cut many long, medium, and short lines. Cut to obscure the sentence meanings.
   d. Medium large size: Cut many long, medium, and short lines. Cut to obscure the sentence meanings.
   e. Large single letter forms: cut one or two only.

2. Place one (or perhaps two) of the large letter forms on 12″ × 14″ white or black background.

3. Build out and around the large letter form with parts of the lines of letters to create a dense massing of letters which will begin to create a textured/patterned effect that also generates a moderate undulating movement.

4. Continue to add small to medium-large letters.

5. At no time should the viewer be aware of sentences or content, as the cut-out letter forms are to be used to create abstract textures and patterns.

6. Work to create easy transitions from size to size; keep abrupt changes of scale to a minimum.

7. This is an additive process that allows for change and alteration as the composition evolves.

Materials:

Construction paper: white or black
Magazines or newspapers
Scissors and exacto-knife
   Warning: Use extreme caution when working with sharp instruments.
White glue

Outcomes:

—Develop the importance of scale, transition, undulating movement, pattern, and texture.
—Learn to see letter forms as abstract shapes, patterns, and textures apart from content.
—Create a rhythmic, arresting composition of a variety of sizes of letter forms.
—Maintain a flexible attitude toward an evolving design process in contrast to a preplanned idea.

Text References:

Discussion of texture and pattern, pp. 65–68
Use of letter forms as design, pp. 182 (upper), 184

An experiment changing the symbolic meaning of
letter forms.

Response and Expression

Four Seasons Sun Symbol

Task:

Design a sun symbol which, with a change of colors, will express the feelings associated with spring, summer, fall, and winter.

1. Develop a sun symbol that is composed of a number of separate shapes. Consider size, contour and edge relationships of the individual shapes in order to create a unified and interesting total shape..

2. Divide a 9″ × 18″ horizontal board into four equal areas and transfer the same design to each area.

3. Select hue, value, and intensity of colors to create the mood of the four seasons. Consider color associations of seasonal changes in the landscape and other dimensions of color such as warmth and coolness that can be used to create mood. Paint the background of each of the sun areas to enhance the feeling of each season.

Materials:

Lay-out paper and tracing paper
Illustration board
Pencil and brushes
Opaque water-based paint
Ruling pen and ruling compass
Straightedge and French curve

Outcomes:

—Learn to use color to create mood.
—Increase awareness of the subjective nature of color.
—Extend the imagination to create symbols that express clearly and give form to a concept or idea.

Text References:

Historical and contemporary sun symbols, pp. 104, 105

Response and Expression

The sun symbol—an experiment in symbol and meaning.

Mood Collage

Task:

Using magazine collage, design a dominantly linear composition which captures a whimsical feeling in color, line, and texture.

1. Experiment with moving, shifting, and trimming the collage pieces to achieve a light, playful effect.

2. Use white or light-value illustration board as a background, size 10″ × 12″.

3. When collage arrangement has been adjusted and refined, adhere the collage pieces to the board with white glue.

Outcomes:

—Learn to create mood with carefully selected line and color passages, enriched by textural areas.
—Experiment with trial-and-error method of problem-solving.

Text References:

Communication of visual ideas, pp. 88–93
Communication through symbol, p. 109

Materials:

Magazine collage
Illustration board
Sissors and exacto-knife
   Warning: Use extreme caution when working with sharp instruments.
Glue

A collage expressing mood through color and shape.

Bibliography

Albers, Anni. *On Weaving*. Middletown, Connecticut: Wesleyan University Press, 1965.
————. *On Designing*. Middletown, Connecticut: Wesleyan University Press, 1971.
Albers, Josef. *Interaction of Color*. New Haven: Yale University Press, 1963.
Anderson, Donald M. *Elements of Design*. New York: Holt, Rinehart & Winston, 1961.
————. *The Art of Written Forms: The Theory & Practice of Calligraphy*. New York: Holt, Rinehart & Winston, 1969.
Applegate, Judith and Varian, Elayne. *Art Deco*. New York: Finch College Museum of Art, 1970.
Arakawa, Hirokazu, et al. *Traditions in Japanese Design*. Tokyo, Japan — Palo Alto, California: Kodansha International, 1967.
Arnheim, Rudolf. *Art and Visual Perception*. Berkeley: University of California Press, 1965.
————. *Visual Thinking*. Berkeley: University of California Press, 1969.
Ballinger, Louise and Broman, T. *Design: Sources and Resources*. New York: Reinhold Publishing Corporation, 1965.
Banham, Reyner. *Theory and Design in the First Machine Age*. London: The Architectural Press, 1960.
Bayer, Herbert, Gropius, Walter, and Gropius, Ise. *Bauhaus 1919–1928*. Boston: Charles T. Branford Company, 1952.
Berenson, Bernard. *Seeing and Knowing*. Greenwich, Connecticut: New York Graphic, 1968.
Bevlin, Marjorie. *Design Through Discovery*. 3rd ed. New York: Holt, Rinehart & Winston, 1977.
Birren, Faber. *Light, Color, Environment*. New York: Van Nostrand Reinhold, 1969.
Blake, Peter. *God's Own Junkyard*. New York: Holt, Rinehart & Winston, Inc., 1964.
Bφe, Alf. *From Gothic Revival to Functional Form*. Oslo: Oslo University Press, 1957.
Bradley, Scully ed. *The Arts in Renewal*. New York: A. S. Barnes Inc., 1951.

Brodatz, Philip. *Textures: A Photographic Album for Artists and Designers*. New York: Dover, 1966.
————. *Wood and Wood Grains: A Photographic Album for Artists and Designers*. New York: Dover, 1972.
Cataldo, John. *Graphic Design*. Scranton: International Textbook Co., 1966.
Collier, Graham. *Form, Space and Vision*. 3rd ed. Englewood Cliffs, New Jersey: Prentice-Hall, 1972.
Constantine, Albert. *Know Your Woods*. New York: Scribner, 1972.
Constantine, Mildred and Larsen, Jack Lenor, *Beyond Craft: The Art Fabric*. New York: Van Nostrand Reinhold, 1972.
De Sausmarez, Maurice. *Basic Design*. New York: Reinhold Publishing Corp., 1964.
Dewey, John. *Art as Experience*. New York: G. P. Putnam's Sons, 1958.
DeZurko, Robert Edward. *Origins of the Functionalist Theory*. New York: Columbia University Press, 1957.
Diamonstein, Barbara Lee. *American Architecture Now II*. New York: Rizzoli International Publications, Inc., 1985.
Dondis, Donis A. *A Primer of Visual Literacy*. Cambridge, Massachusetts: M.I.T. Press, 1973.
Downer, Marion. *The Story of Design*. New York: Lothrop, Lee and Shepard Co., Inc., 1963.
Drexler, Arthur and Daniel, Greta. *Introduction to Twentieth Century Design*. New York: The Museum of Modern Art, 1959.
Dreyfus, Henry. *Industrial Design*. A Progress Report — 1929–1952. New York and Los Angeles: Henry Dreyfus, 1952.
————. *Designing for People*. New York: Simon Schuster, Inc., 1955.
Duerdon, Dennis. *African Art*. London: Hamlyn Publishing Group Ltd., 1968.
Ehrenzweig, Anton. *The Hidden Order of Art*. Berkeley: University of California Press, 1967.

Ellinger, R. *Color, Structure and Design*. New York: Van Nostrand Reinhold, 1980.
Evans, Helen M. *Man The Designer*. New York: The MacMillan Co., 1973.
Farr, Michael. *Design in British Industry*. Cambridge, England: Cambridge University Press, 1955.
Faulkner, Ray and Ziegfeld, Edwin. *Art Today*. 5th ed. New York: Holt, Rinehart and Winston, 1974.
Friedman, Wm. ed. *Twentieth Century Design U.S.A.* Hollingpress, 1959–60.
Fry, Roger. *Vision & Design*. New York: Brentanos, 1924.
Gardner, John. *Self-Renewal*. New York: Harper and Row, 1965.
Garrett, Lillian. *Visual Design — A Problem Solving Approach*. New York: Reinhold, 1967.
Gatto, Joseph A., Porter, Albert, and Selleck, John. *Exploring Visual Design*. Worcester, Massachusetts: Davis Publications, Inc., 1978.
Giedion, Siegfried. *Mechanization Takes Command*. New York: Oxford University Press, 1952.
————. *Walter Gropius: Team and Teamwork*. New York: Reinhold Publishing Corp., 1954.
————. *Space, Time and Architecture*. 3rd ed. Cambridge, Massachusetts: Harvard University Press, 1956.
Goldberger, Paul. *On the Rise*. New York: New York Times Book Co., Inc., 1983.
Graves, Maitland. *The Art of Color & Design*. New York: McGraw-Hill, 1951.
Greenough, Horatio. *Form and Function*. Edited by Harold A. Small. Berkeley: University of California Press, 1936.
Gregory, Robert. *The Intelligent Eye*. San Francisco: McGraw-Hill Book Co., 1970.
Grillo, Paul. *Form, Function and Design*. New York: Dover, 1975.
Halland, Laurence B. ed. *Who Designs America*. New York: Doubleday & Co., Inc., 1966.

Henderson, Philip. *William Morris: His Life, Work & Friends.* New York: McGraw-Hill Book Company, 1967.

Hillebrand, Henri ed. *Graphic Designers in the USA/1.* New York: Universe Books, 1971.

Hillier, Bevis. *The Decorative Arts of the Forties and Fifties.* New York: Clarkson N. Potter, Inc., 1975.

Hofman, Armin. *Graphic Design Manual: Principles & Practice.* New York: Van Nostrand Reinhold Company, 1965.

Hollander, Harry. *Plastics for Jewelry.* New York: Watson-Guptill, 1974.

Horn, Richard. *Memphis Objects, Furniture and Patterns.* Philadelphia, Pennsylvania: Running Press/Quarto, 1985.

Hulme, F. E., et al. *Art Studies from Nature, as Applied to Design for the Use of Architects, Designers, and Manufacturers.* London: Virtue and Company, 1872.

Itten, Johannes. *The Art of Color.* New York: Van Nostrand Reinhold, 1974.

—————. *Design and Form.* 2nd rev. ed. New York: Van Nostrand Reinhold, 1975.

Iwamiya, Takeji. *Design & Craftsmanship of Japan.* New York: Henry N. Abrams, Inc., 1963.

Jacobsen, E. ed. *Trademark Design.* Chicago: Paul Theobald, 1952.

Jencks, Charles. *The Language of Post-Modern Architecture.* 3rd ed. New York: Rizzoli International Publications, Inc., 1981.

Jencks, Charles. *Post-Modern Classicism.* London: Architectural Design, 1980.

Jung, Carl G. *Man and His Symbols.* New York: Doubleday & Co., Inc. 1964.

Kaufman, Edgar, Jr. *What is Modern Design?* New York: The Museum of Modern Art, 1950.

Kepes, Gyorgy. *Language of Vision.* Chicago: Paul Theobald, 1944.

—————. ed. *Education of Vision.* New York: Braziller, 1965.

—————. *The New Landscape.* Chicago: Paul Theobold & Company, 1967.

—————. ed. *Arts of the Environment.* New York: Braziller, 1972.

Klotz, Heinrich. *The History of Postmodern Architecture.* Cambridge, Massachusetts: MIT Press, 1988.

Koch, Robert. *Louis C. Tiffany, Rebel in Glass.* New York: Crown Publishers, Inc., 1966.

Kojiro, Yuichiro. *Forms in Japan.* Honolulu: East-West Center Press, 1965.

Kranz, S. and Fisher, R. *The Design Continuum.* New York: Reinhold Publishing Corp., 1966.

Kron, John and Slesin, Suzanne. *High Tech.* New York: Clarkson N. Potter, Inc., 1978.

Langer, Suzanne. *Feeling and Form.* New York: Scribner, 1953.

Larrabee, Eric and Vignelli, Massimo. *Knoll Design.* New York: Harry N. Abrams, Inc., 1981.

Leach, Bernard. *A Potter's Book.* Levit-Town, New York: Transatlantic Arts, 1965.

Lenning, Henry F. *The Art Nouveau.* The Hague: Martinus Nijhoff, 1951.

Lichten, Frances. *The Decorative Art of Victoria's Era.* New York: Charles Scribner's Sons, 1950.

Lingstrom, Freda. *The Seeing Eye.* London: Studio Books, 1960.

Lowry, Bates. *The Visual Experience.* Englewood Cliffs, New Jersey: Prentice-Hall, 1965.

Mackail, John William. *The Life of William Morris.* 2 vols. London, New York and Toronto: Longmans, Green and Company, 1911.

Madsen, S. Tschudi. *Art Nouveau.* New York: McGraw-Hill Book Co., Inc., 1967.

McHarg, Ian. *Design With Nature.* Garden City, New York: Natural History Press, 1969.

McKim, Robert. *Experience in Visual Thinking.* Monterrey, California: Brooks/Cole, 1972.

McQuiston, Liz. *Women in Design.* New York: Rizzoli International Publications, Inc., 1988.

Moholy-Nagy, Laszlo. *Vision in Motion.* Chicago: Paul Theobald, 1947.

—————. *The New Vision.* New York: Geo. Wittenborn, 1949.

Moholy-Nagy, Sibylle. *Native Genius in American Architecture.* New York: Horizon Press, 1957.

—————. *Moholy-Nagy, Experiment in Totality.* New York: Harper and Brothers, 1950.

Morris, William. *Hopes and Fears for Art. Lectures on Art and Industry.* Vol. XXII: The Collected Works of William Morris. London: Longmans, Green and Company, 1904.

Morton, Philip. *Contemporary Jewelry.* 2nd ed. New York: Holt, Rinehart and Winston, 1976.

Moseley, Spencer, Johnson, Pauline, and Koenig, Hazel. *Crafts Design.* Belmont, California: Wadsworth Publications Co., 1962.

Mumford, Lewis. *Technics and Civilization.* New York: Harcourt, Brace & Co., 1944.

—————. *The Condition of Man.* New York: Harcourt, Brace & Co., 1944.

Munsell, Albert H. *A Color Notation.* Baltimore, Maryland: Munsell Color Co., Inc., 1946.

Naylor, Gillian. *The Bauhaus.* New York: E. P. Dutton & Co., Inc., 1968.

—————. *The Arts and Crafts Movement.* Cambridge, Massachusetts: The M.I.T. Press, 1971.

Nelson, George. *Problems of Design.* New York: Whitney, 1965.

Neutra, Richard. *Survival Through Design.* New York: Oxford University Press, 1954.

Newman, Thelma. *Plastics as an Art Form.* rev. ed. Philadelphia: Chilton, 1969.

—————. *Plastics as Design Form.* Philadelphia: Chilton, 1972.

Newton, Norman T. *An Approach to Design.* Reading, Massachusetts: Addison-Wesley Press, 1951.

Ocvirk, Otto G., Bone, Robert O., Stinson, Robert E. and Wigg, Phillip R. *Art Fundamentals: Theory and Practice.* 3rd ed. Dubuque, Iowa: Wm. Brown, 1975.

Pearson, Katherine. *American Crafts.* New York: Stewart, Tabori and Chang Publishers, Inc., 1983.

Pearson, Ralph. *The New Art Education.* New York: Harper, 1953.

—————. *How to See Modern Pictures.* New York: Dial Press, 1925.

Peter, John. *Design With Glass.* New York: Reinhold Publishing Corp., 1964.

Pevsner, Nikolaus. *The Sources of Modern Architecture and Design.* New York: Frederick A. Praeger, 1968.

—————. *Pioneers of Modern Design: From William Morris to Walter Gropius.* New York: The Museum of Modern Art, 1949.

Portoghesi, Paolo. *PostModern.* New York: Rizzoli International Publications, Inc., 1983.

Rand, Paul. *Thoughts on Design.* New York: Van Nostrand Reinhold, 1970.

Rathbone, Richard A. *Introduction to Functional Design.* New York: McGraw-Hill Book Co., 1950.

Ratia, Armi ed. in chief. *The Ornamo Book of Finnish Design.* Helsinki: 1962.

Read, Herbert. *Art and Industry: The Principles of Industrial Design.* New York: Horizon Press, 1954.

Rees, David. *Creative Plastics.* New York: Viking, 1973.

Renner, Paul. *Color, Order and Harmony.* New York: Reinhold Publishing Corp., 1965.

Ritchie, James. *Design in Nature.* New York: Scribner, 1937.

Rottger, Ernst. *Creative Wood Design.* New York: Reinhold Publishing Corp., 1961.

Rowe, William. *Original Art Deco Designs.* New York: Dover Publications, Inc., 1973.

Sargent, Walter. *The Enjoyment and Use of Color.* New York: Dover Publications, Inc., 1964.

Schaefer, Herwin. *Nineteenth Century Modern.* New York: Praeger Publishers, 1970.

Schmutzler, Robert. *Art Nouveau.* New York: Harry N. Abrams, Inc. 1978.

Seltz, Peter and Constantine, Mildred. *Art Nouveau.* Garden City, New York: Doubleday Co., Inc., 1959.

Shahn, Ben. *Love and Joy About Letters.* New York: Grossman, 1963.

Slivka, Rose. *The Crafts in the Modern World.* New York: Horizon Press, 1968.

Society of Industrial Designers. *Industrial Design in America, 1954.* New York: Farrar, Straus and Young, 1954.

Solberg, Ramona. *Inventive Jewelry Making.* New York: Van Nostrand Reinhold, Co., 1972.

Sommer, Robert. *Design Awareness.* New York: Holt, Rinehart & Winston, 1972.

Straghe, Wolf. *Forms and Patterns in Nature.* New York: Ballantine, 1972.

Teague, Walter Darwin. *Design This Day.* New York: Harcourt, Brace and Company, 1940.

Trowell, Margaret. *African Design.* New York: Praeger Publishers, 1966.

Venturi, Robert. *Complexity and Contradiction in Architecture.* New York: Museum of Modern Art, 1966.

Vernon, M. D. *The Psychology of Perception.* Middlesex, England: Penguin Books Ltd., 1971.

Watkinson, Ray. *William Morris as Designer.* New York: Reinhold Publishing Corp., 1967.

Wingler, Hans M. *Graphic Work from the Bauhaus.* Greenwich, Connecticut: New York Graphic, 1969.

Wolfe, Tom. *From Bauhaus to Our House.* New York: Farrar, Straus & Giroux, 1981.

Wong, Wucius. *Principles of Two Dimensional Design.* New York: Van Nostrand Reinhold, 1972.

Index

Abstraction, 28
Aesthetic
  expression, 88
  imagination, 23
  order, 33
  perception, 7
After image, 55
Albers, Anni, 160
Albers, Joseph, 127, 135, 152
Albert Memorial, 119
Alteration, 25
Alternation, 83
Analogous, 55
Architects Collaborative, The, 128
Arnheim, Rudolf, 5, 9, 28
Art
  Celtic, 123
  cybernetic, 135
  Deco, 19, 89, 90, 92, 94, 131
  exotic, 124
  folk, 66
  Greek, 74
  Japanese, 40, 82, 124
  Nouveau, 19, 81, 83, 92, 99–103
  primitive, 66
Arts and Crafts Movement, 120
Attraction, 76

Balance, 81
  informal, 81
Barcelona chair, 128, 151
Barron, Frank, 7
Bass, Saul, 175
Bassett, Florence Schust Knoll, 173
Bauhaus, 4, 95, 127, 135
Bayer, Herbert, 161
Beardsley, Aubrey, 124, 150
Bentwood, 143
Blake, William, 124
Bon Marché, 133
Brainstorming, 26, 73
Brandt, Marianne, 156
Breuer, Marcel, 128, 164

Caroll, Lewis, 5
Cassandre, A. M., 163
Chiaroscuro, 43
Chwast, Seymour, 178
Clarification, 113
Cole, Henry, 119
Color, 45, 87
  additive, 46
  composition, 52
  harmony, 52
  symbolism, 56
Communication, 105
  nonverbal, 107
  verbal, 107
Complementary, 52
Contour, 36
Contrast, 40, 76
Crystal Palace, 119

Da Vinci, Leonardo, 23
Design
  elements of, 35
  environmental, 126
  industrial, 155
  Moslem, 31
  process, 87, 92
  solution, 101
Dewey, John, 9
Draftsman, 35
Dreyfus, Henry, 165

Eames, Charles and Ray, 169
Electronic images, 31
Emphasis, 76
Environmental
  design, 126
  images, 16
Escher, M.C., 59
Expression, 91
Expressionism, 91
Eye movement, 78

Fashion, 115
Fauvist, 91

Ferroconcrete, 128
Form, 60
Formal, 81
Fovea centralis, 24
Function, 99

Gardner, John, 26
Gehry, Frank, 142
Girard, Alexander, 167
Glaser, Milton, 179
Golden mean, 74
Gothic, 124
Graffiti, 105
Graphic Expressionism, 174
Graphics, 136
Graves, Michael, 142
Gray, Eileen, 159
Gropius, Walter, 95, 127, 135

Handcrafting, 133
Haring, Hugo, 135
Herdeg, Walter, 136
High tech, 138
Hopper, Bruce, 181
Hue, 48
Human
  made environment, 36
  scale, 165

Illusion, 36
Imagery, 5
Imagination, 5
  creative, 23
Insight, 4
Intelligence, 9
Intensity, 49
International style, 151
Intuition, 8
Inversion, 85
Itten, Johannes, 127, 135, 153
Ives, Herbert E., 50

Jabberwock, 5
Johnson, Philip, 135

Kepes, Gyorgy, 135, 166
Knoll Associates, 173

Lacquer, 133
Lalique, René, 133
Language systems, 107
Larsen, Jack Lenor, 177
Left brain hemisphere, 26
Line, 35
  qualities, 36
Linear perspective, 69
Loewy, Raymond, 155
London Transport, 133
Lubalin, Herb, 174

Mackintosh, Charles Renni, 149
Mackmurdo, Arthur H., 146
Maison de L'art Noveau, 123
Mass produced,135
McKim, Robert, 7
Matisse, Henri, 91
Memphis Design, 147
Modern Movement, 131
Moholy-Nagy, Lazlo, 127, 135, 158
Monochromatic, 52
Morris, William, 120, 144
Motivation, 88
Movement, 78
Mucha, Alphonse, 147
Munsell, Albert (color system), 50

Nelson, George, 170
Newton, Norman, 89, 91
Newton, Sir Isaac, 45
Nitsche, Eric, 12
Notan, 40

Ostwald, Wilhelm, 50

Pattern, 68, 82
Paxton, John, 119
Pearson, Ralph, 9
Perception, 5, 7, 15
Perceptive eye, 9
Perspective
  aerial, 69
Picasso, 35
Pictographs, 107
Pigment, 48
Poiret, Paul, 131
Pop Art, 139
Post-Modern, 139
Problem solving, 1, 111
Proportion, 73
Push Pin Studios, 178

Radial, 81, 82
Radiation, 85
Rand, Paul, 172
Recorded images, 19

Refinement, 113
Renaissance, 35
Repetition, 83
Research, 113
Resolution, 113
Retina, 24
Rhythm, 83
Rhythmic movement, 78
Right brain hemisphere, 26
Rococo, 124
Ruskin, John, 127

Selection, 24
Sequential images, 78
Shahn, Ben, 159
Shape, 58
  and form, 58
  negative, 58
Silhouette, 58
Simplification, 25
Simulated texture, 66
Sottsass, Ettore, 182
Space, 69, 87
  illusionary, 78
  negative, 71
  positive, 69
Space arts, 69
Spatial field, 69
Spontaneity, 26, 62
Spontaneous, 64
  trial, 73, 111
Style, 115
Subtractive color, 46
Surface, 69
Swiss, 138
Symbolism, 31, 69, 105
Symmetry, 74
Synthetics, 135

Tactile, 65
Tanaka, Ikko, 180
Technology, 101
Tenebrism, 43
Texture, 65
  invented, 66
Thonet, Michael, 143
Tiffany, Louis Comfort, 123, 145
Triad, 55
Truth to materials, 95
Tutankhamen's tomb, 131

Value, 40, 48
van der Rohe, Ludwig Mies, 151
van de Velde, Henry, 148
Venturi, Robert, 142
Vernon, M. D., 8
Victoria (Queen of England), 117
Victoria and Albert Museum, 120
Victorian, 115, 117
Video artists, 31
Visibility, 40

Vision
  curious, 11
  imaginative, 11
  practical, 11
  pure, 11, 12
Visual
  awareness, 101
  field, 76
  imagination, 23
  intake, 7
  research, 15, 16, 19
  structure, 91
  symbols, 105
  thinking, 3
  vocabulary, 33, 35

Wegner, Hans, 171
Whistler, James A., 124
Whitney, John, 135
Wolfe, Tom, 135

PHOTOGRAPHIC ACKNOWLEDGMENTS

Page 2. House in Nerima Tokyo by Itsuko Hasegawa. Courtesy of the architect.

Page 6. Logo Design. Courtesy Hungry Tiger Inc., Van Nuys, California.

Page 10. Illustration for a story entitled "Bluebottle" in *Show* Magazine. Courtesy of the artist. Milton Glaser.

Page 14. Genre Luristan pot, Iran, 850–780 B.C. Courtesy of Los Angeles County Museum of Art: Gift of Nasli M. Heeramaneck.

Page 21. Head of Orpheus. Coptic fragment, Egypt, fourth or fifth century. Courtesy of Los Angeles County Museum of Art.

Page 21. Mask of rain god Tlaloc, Mixtec Culture, Mexico, 900–1200 A.D. Courtesy of Honolulu Academy of Arts.

Page 21. "Ichikawa Ebizo as Takemura Sadanoshin" by Toshusai Sharaku 1794, Japan. Courtesy of Honolulu Academy of Arts, The James A. Michener Collection.

Page 29. Wooden duck. Courtesy of Dextra Frankel.

Page 30. Navajo rug. Courtesy of Dextra Frankel.

Page 30. Pottery Bowl, Acoma Tribe, American Indian. Courtesy of Dextra Frankel.

Page 31. Jug, Persian, Kashan early 13th Century. Courtesy of Los Angeles County Museum of Art: The Nasli M. Heeramaneck Collection, gift of Joan Palevsky.

Page 34. Logo Design, Honolulu Symphony Society. Courtesy of the designer, Bruce Hopper.

Page 37. Newspaper ad. Courtesy of Frank Brothers, Long Beach, California.

Page 38. Abstract sketch. Courtesy of the artist, George James.

Page 38. Sketch of horse. Courtesy of the artist, George James.

Page 39. Figure with caged head. Courtesy of the artist, George James.

Page 42. Blanket. Tlingit. Artist Mary Ebbets Hunt. Southeastern Alaska. Late 19th century. Courtesy of Honolulu Academy of Arts.

Page 42. "Island Vibes," record album, Designer Ellis Applebaum. Courtesy of Gordon Broad. Publisher.

Page 49. Stitchery. Courtesy of the designer, Esther Feldman.

Page 49. Two designs by Edouard Benedictus. Courtesy Crescent Books.

Page 54. Two designs by Edouard Benedictus. Courtesy Crescent Books.

Page 57. Needlepoint. Courtesy of the designer, Esther Feldman.

Page 57. A design by Edouard Benedictus. Courtesy Crescent Books.

Page 59. "Sky and Water" by M. C. Escher, © Beeldrecht, Amsterdam/VAGA, New York Collection Haags Gemeentemuseum—The Hague, 1981.

Page 62. Japanese Combs. Courtesy of Dextra Frankel.

Page 63. Deer. Iran, c. 1200 B.C. Courtesy of Los Angeles County Museum of Art: Gift of Nasli M. Heeramaneck.

Page 65. Silver pitcher. Courtesy of the designer-craftsman, Al Ching.

Page 66. Raku Platter. Courtesy of the designer-craftsman, Paul Soldner.

Page 66. Fiber Hanging. Designer/craftswoman Julie Connell. Courtesy California State University, Fullerton Art Gallery.

Page 67. Cartoon. Courtesy of the artist, Don Reilly. © 1978 *The New Yorker Magazine, Inc.*

Page 71. Detroit Lions Team Poster. Illustrator Chuck Ren, © 1980 NFL Properties, Inc.

Page 71. "Music Garden," an illustration. Courtesy of the artist, Milton Glaser.

Page 76. Illustration for *Signature* Magazine. Courtesy of the artist, Seymour Chwast.

Page 80. Dahomey figures. Courtesy of Dextra Frankel.

Page 86. "Crossing" by Carol Shaw-Sutton. Courtesy of Craft and Folk-Art Museum, Los Angeles. Exhibit: "Made in L.A.: Contemporary Crafts 1981." Photographer Roger Marshutz.

Page 90. Jefferson Starship "Dragon Fly" album cover. Illustrator Peter Lloyd, © 1974, RCA Records.

Page 93. "The States" Album cover. Illustrator: Shusei Nagaoka. Art Director/Designer: Bill Murphy of Rod Dyer, Inc., Courtesy Bill Murphy.

Page 94. Bone construction, Ainu. Courtesy of Dextra Frankel.

Page 97. Dough figure. Courtesy of the designer, Dextra Frankel.

Page 97. Storage Unit. Courtesy of the designer, Dextra Frankel.

Page 100. Rocking Chair. Courtesy of the designer/craftsman, Sam Maloof.

Page 105. Cartoon. Courtesy of the artist, Bob Weber. © 1969, *The New Yorker Magazine, Inc.*

Page 109. Logo, Minnesota Zoo. Courtesy of Minnesota Zoological Garden.

Page 109. Logo, Hartford Whalers. Courtesy of Hartford Whalers Hockey Club.

Page 109. Logo, Northwest Airlines. Courtesy of Northwest Airlines, Inc.

Page 109. Logo, Fuji Golf Club. Courtesy of the designer, Bruce Hopper.

Page 109. Logo, Honsador Lumber Firm. Courtesy of the designer, Bruce Hopper.

Page 109. Logo, Ala Moana Dental Group. Courtesy of the designer, Bruce Hopper.

Page 109. Logo, CBS. Courtesy of CBS, Inc.

Page 121. Victorian Pincushion. Courtesy of Dextra Frankel.

Page 121. Stamped Mail Purse. Courtesy of Dextra Frankel.

Page 122. Decorative letter forms from *The Studio* and *Art et Décoration*, courtesy of the Dover Pictorial Archive.

Page 130. The Wassily Tubular Chair, designer Marcel Breuer. Courtesy of Knoll International, Inc., U.S.A.

Page 133. Eames Residence by Charles & Ray Eames. Photograph by Julius Shulman Inc., Los Angeles, California.

Page 134. Armchair. Chrome-plated steel wire, naugahyde. 29¼" h. 1952. Designer Harry Bertoia. Courtesy Collection of The Museum of Modern Art, New York. Gift of the manufacturer, Knoll Associates, Inc., U.S.A.

Page 143. Teapot by Ken Horvath. Courtesy of the artist.

Page 145. The Denise arm chair by Nathalie du Pasquier. Courtesy of the artist.

Page 146. The Memphis Clock by Nathalie du Pasquier. Courtesy of the artist.

Page 146. The Athena Chair. Courtesy of The Wicker Works.

Page 150. Rocking Chair, Michael Thonet. Courtesy of the Brooklyn Museum, Caroline A. L. Pratt Fund.

Page 152. Pimpernel Wallpaper, Designer William Morris. Courtesy of Victoria and Albert Museum, London, England.

Page 152. Plaque "Favrile" glass by Louis Comfort Tiffany. Courtesy of the Metropolitan Museum of Art, New York City. Gift of H. O. Havemeyer, 1896. All rights reserved, the Metropolitan Museum of Art.

Page 155. Title Page for *Wren's City Churches* by Arthur Mackmurdo. Courtesy of Victoria and Albert Museum, London, England.

Page 155. Menu design by Alphonse Mucha, © Spadem, Paris/VAGA, New York, 1982.

Page 156. Chair by Charles Rennie Mackintosh. A reprint from the C. R. Mackintosh Designs Catalog, 1979. Courtesy The Seibu Museum of Art.

Page 158. Drawing, "J'ai Baisé to Bouche Jokanaan," by Aubrey Beardsley. Courtesy of Princeton University Library.

Page 160. Barcelona Chair by Ludwig Mies Van der Rohe. Courtesy of Knoll International, Inc., U.S.A.

Page 162. Light-Dark Composition by Johannes Itten, from *The Elements of Color* by Johannes Itten, © 1970 by Otto Maier Verlag. Reprinted by permission of Van Nostrand Reinhold Co.

Page 163. Avanti, Designer Raymond Loewy, Courtesy of Avanti Motor Corporation, Photograph by David R. Walton.

Page 165. Teapot. Nickel silver, ebony. 3⅜" h. 1924. Designer Marianne Brandt. Courtesy Collection of The Museum of Modern Art, New York. Phyllis B. Lambert Fund.

Page 169. Woven Silk Tapestry by Anni Albers. Reprinted from *The Bauhaus* by Hans M. Wingler by permission of the MIT Press, Cambridge, Massachusetts. English adaptation © 1969 by the Massachusetts Institute of Technology.

Page 169. Exhibition Stand by Herbert Bayer. Reprinted from *The Bauhaus* by Hans M. Wingler by permission of the MIT Press, Cambridge, Massachusetts. English adaptation © 1969 by the Massachusetts Institute of Technology.

Page 172. Control Console Diagram by Henry Dreyfuss, from *Designing for People* by Henry Dreyfuss, © 1955, 1967, by Henry Dreyfuss. Reprinted by permission of Viking Penguin, Inc.

Page 174. Rhythmic Light Mural by Gyorgy Kepes. Reprinted from *The Bauhaus* by Hans M. Wingler by permission of the MIT Press, Cambridge, Massachusetts. English adaptation © 1969 by the Massachusetts Institute of Technology.

Page 174. Woven Casement Cloth, designed by Alexander Girard, from *Fabrics for Interiors* by Jack Lenor Larsen and Jeanne Weeks, © 1975 by Van Nostrand Reinhold Co. Reprinted by permission of the publisher.

Page 176. Dining Chair, designed by the office of Charles and Ray Eames.

Page 179. Chair, designed by architect Hans J. Wegner and cabinetmaker Johannes Hansen.

Page 180. Trademark, TV Billboard, Westinghouse, designed by Paul Rand, from *Thoughts on Design* by Paul Rand, © 1970 by Studio Vista Limited. Reprinted by permission of Van Nostrand Reinhold Company.

Page 180. Detail, the New York showroom of Knoll Inc., designed by Florence Schust Knoll Bassett. Courtesy of Knoll Associates, Inc., U.S.A.

Page 182. Sudler, Hennessey, & Lubalin Logo designed by Herb Lubalin. Finished Lettering by John Pistilli. Courtesy of Sudler and Hennessey, Inc.

Page 184. Catalog design for Pyramid Films by Saul Bass. Courtesy of Pyramid Film and Video, California.

Page 185. Fabric, "Interplay". Courtesy of the designer, Jack Lenor Larsen.

Page 186. Letter "A". Courtesy of the designer, Seymour Chwast.

Page 186. Letter "A". Courtesy of the designer, Milton Glaser.

Page 188. Trademark, Hanae Mori Knit. Courtesy of the designer, Ikko Tanaka.

A number of the photographs which appear in *Design Dialogue* are from the authors' private collections and are believed not to be the subject of claimed copyright. If copyright is claimed for any of these, the authors will be pleased to correspond with the claimant and to make an appropriate arrangement.